WHAT JESUS TAUGHT

The Sayings Translated and Arranged
With Expository Commentary

BURTON SCOTT EASTON

THE ABINGDON PRESS
NEW YORK   CINCINNATI   CHICAGO

Copyright, 1938, by
BURTON SCOTT EASTON

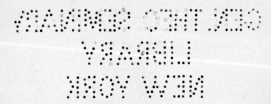
Printed in the United States of America

CONTENTS

PREFACE

THIS collection of Jesus' sayings is designed primarily for those who do not care to follow the intricacies of modern Gospel criticism and who wish only the firm ground of "assured" results. The principle of selection, therefore, has not been the editor's own preference but the general consensus of present-day opinion; with a greater readiness to omit rather than to include debated passages. The most disputed subjects are those of the Messianic consciousness and the apocalyptic language; here such contradictory opinions are held that no choice of material will be universally satisfactory. But much of this controversy is based on premises that are more theological than historical; and every passage printed (perhaps apart from those marked a, b, c at the beginning) has the support of specialists who otherwise hold radical views. Apart from these subjects there are few serious scholars who will not agree that Jesus' actual teaching is summarized with reasonable accuracy by the collection as a whole.

Quite aside from critical problems, however, this collection may be used simply as a compilation of representative passages from the first three Gospels, to serve as an introduction to the fuller study of the Gospels themselves. For the first century the arrangement of Jesus' sayings as given by the Evangelists was ideal; but for us today the appeal of these sayings is often more direct when detached from their Gospel context and given separately. The poetic structure that Jesus deliberately gave much of His teaching has been restored, and will often make the meaning clear without further explanation. The translation largely retains the familiar wording of the traditional English versions, although in some instances wide departures have been necessary to convey the original meaning. In making this translation the researches of specialists in the Greek text and—especially—of experts in the Aramaic language have been freely used.

Explicit quotations from the Old Testament are printed in italics. Since Old Testament language was archaic in Jesus' day, in these quotations the traditional English Biblical style has been retained.

The comments have been reduced to the briefest dimensions possible; their sole purpose is to remove difficulties due to our remoteness from the events and so to place the reader as nearly as possible in the immediate presence of Jesus.

BURTON SCOTT EASTON.

General Theological Seminary,
New York City.

THE PREPARATION

THE BAPTIST

a John the Baptist preached a baptism of repentance for the remission of sins. And he said to the people: Repent!
For the Kingdom of God is at hand.

You children of vipers!
  Who has warned you to flee from the coming wrath?
Show the fruits of the repentance you profess,
  And do not begin to say, "Abraham is our father";
    For I tell you that out of these stones,
    God can create children of Abraham.
Already the ax is lying at the root of the trees,
  And any tree that does not produce good fruits,
  Will be cut down and cast into the fire.
I, to be sure, am baptizing you with water:
  But One is coming who is mightier than I,
    The thong of whose sandals I am not fit to unfasten,
He will baptize you with holy Spirit and with fire!
His winnowing shovel is in his hand,
  And he will thoroughly clean his threshing floor;
The wheat he will gather into his storehouse,
  But the chaff he will burn with unquenchable fire.

JESUS' BAPTISM

b Jesus was baptized by John in the river Jordan. And as he came up out of the water, he saw the heavens opened and the Spirit descending upon him like a dove. And a Voice came from heaven, saying:
Thou art my Son, my Beloved, my Chosen One.

7

THE TEMPTATION

c   The Spirit led Jesus into the wilderness, where he was tempted
by the devil. He was there forty days and forty nights, fasting;
and he grew hungry. And the Tempter said to him, "If you are
the Son of God, command these stones to become bread." But
Jesus answered:

It is written: *Man shall not live by bread alone, but by
every law that God hath proclaimed.*

Then the devil carried him aloft, and showed him all the king-
doms of the world and their glory. And he said, "All these things
I will give you, if you will kneel down and worship me." But
Jesus answered:

It is written: *Thou shalt worship the Lord thy God,
and Him only shalt thou serve.*

Then the devil took him up to the pinnacle of the Temple, and
said: "If you are the Son of God, throw yourself down from here;
since it is written, *He shall give His angels charge over thee; and
they shall bear thee up on their hands, lest haply thou dash thy
foot against a stone.*" But Jesus answered:

It is also written: *Thou shalt not tempt the Lord thy
God.*

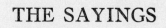

THE SAYINGS

I

RIGHTEOUSNESS
The Way of Righteousness

THE SUPREME STANDARD

1 Jesus was asked, "Which Commandment is first of all?" And he
answered

The first Commandment is:

Hear, O Israel: the Lord our God is one Lord!
And thou shalt love the Lord thy God
With all thy heart,
And with all thy soul,
And with all thy mind,
And with all thy strength.

The second Commandment is:

Thou shalt love thy neighbor as thyself.

2 Think not that I have come to destroy the Law and the
Prophets:

I have not come to destroy, but to enforce them in full:
Whatsoever you would that men should do unto you,
Do you also unto them;

This is the Law and the Prophets!

LOVE OF NEIGHBOR

3 You have heard that it was said,
"*Thou shalt love thy neighbor* and hate thine enemy."
But I say to you,
Love your enemies,
And pray for those who persecute you,
That you may become sons of your Father who is in
heaven.

For He makes His sun to rise on the evil and on the
good,
And sends His rain on the just and on the unjust.

4 If you love those who love you, what reward have you?
Do not the very publicans the same?
And if you greet only your brothers, what reward have
you?
Do not the very heathen the same?
Your love shall be as perfect
As your heavenly Father's love is perfect.

5 If you love those who love you, what thanks have you?
Even sinners love those who love them!
If you do good to those who do good to you, what thanks
have you?
Even sinners do the same!
If you lend to those from whom you hope to receive,
what thanks have you?
Even sinners do the same!
But
Love your enemies,
And do them good,
And lend to them,
Never despairing!
And your reward shall be great,
And you shall be sons of the Most High,
For He is kind to the unthankful and the evil.

6 Jesus was asked, "Who is my neighbor?" And he answered:
A certain man was going down from Jerusalem to
Jericho. And he fell among thieves, who stripped him
and beat him, and went away leaving him half-dead.
And a certain priest chanced to be going down that
way; and when he saw him he passed by on the other
side. And similarly a Levite also, when he came to
the place and saw him, passed by on the other side.
But a certain traveling Samaritan came where he was;

and when he saw him he was moved with pity. And he came to him and bound up his wounds, pouring oil and wine on them. And he set him on his own beast and brought him to an inn, where he took care of him. And on the next day he took out money and gave it to the innkeeper, saying, "Take care of him; and if you spend more than this, I will pay you when I come back again."

Which of these three, do you think, proved "neighbor" to the man who fell among the thieves? He was answered, "The one who was merciful to him." And Jesus said,

Go and do the same!

PRIDE

7 There are last who shall be first,
And there are first who shall be last.

8 He who exalts himself shall be humbled,
And he who humbles himself shall be exalted.

9 Judge not, that you be not judged:
For with what judgment you judge
You shall be judged;
And with what measure you measure
It shall be measured to you.

10 Why do you stare at the mote that is in your brother's
eye,
And do not notice the beam that is in your own eye?
Or how can you say to your brother, "Let me take the
mote out of your eye,"
While, look, there is a beam in your own eye?
You hypocrite!
First take the beam out of your own eye!
And then you can see how to take the mote out of your
brother's eye!

11 If any of you have a servant plowing or feeding cattle,

will he say to him when he comes in from work, "Sit
down at once to your meal"? Will he not rather say,
"Prepare my meal, and serve me while I eat and drink;
then, after I have finished, you may eat and drink"?
And will he thank the servant for obeying his orders?

Just so, when you have done all the things commanded you, say, "We are merely servants; we have
done only what it was our duty to do."

ANGER

12 You have heard that it was said,
    "Thou shalt not kill and whoever kills has guilt de-
        serving the death penalty."
But I say to you,
    Whoever is angry with his brother
        Has guilt deserving the death penalty;
    Whoever abuses his brother
        Has guilt deserving a blasphemer's punishment;
    Whoever curses his brother
        Has guilt deserving burning in the Valley of
        Hinnom.

13   If you are in the act of offering your gift on the altar,
and remember there that your brother has a grievance
against you, leave your gift there in front of the altar!
Go; first be reconciled with your brother; and then
come back and offer your gift.

REVENGE

14 When you pray, say
    Forgive us our trespasses, for we forgive those who
        trespass against us.

15 If you forgive men their trespasses,
    Your heavenly Father will forgive you your tres-
        passes;

But if you do not forgive men their trespasses,
    Neither will your heavenly Father forgive you your
        trespasses.

16 If your brother sin against you, reprove him,
  And if he repent, forgive him.
  And if he sin against you seven times a day,
    And seven times a day turn to you saying, "I repent,"
  You shall forgive him.

17 Peter said to Jesus, "How often shall my brother sin against me
and I forgive him? Until seven times?" Jesus answered:
  Not, "Until seven times,"
  But, "Until seventy times seven."

18 You have heard that it was said,
    "An eye for an eye, and a tooth for a tooth."
  But I say to you,
    Resist not evil:
        If anyone strikes you on the right cheek,
            Turn to him the other also;
        If anyone sues you for your cloak,
            Let him have your coat also;
        If anyone compels you to carry a burden a mile,
            Go with him two.

19 Judge not,
    And you shall not be judged;
  Condemn not,
    And you shall not be condemned;
  Forgive,
    And it shall be forgiven you;
  Give,
    And it shall be given you:
  Good measure, pressed down, shaken together, running
        over, shall be poured into your lap.

20 A Samaritan village would not receive him; and his disciples
asked, "Sir, do you wish that we should command fire to come
down out of heaven and destroy them?"
  But he turned and rebuked them.

21   The Kingdom of God is like a king, who undertook to
settle accounts with his servants. And as the settle-
ment began, a man was brought to him who owed him
ten thousand talents. But he was unable to pay; so
his master ordered him to be sold, with his wife and
his children and all that he had, that payment might
be made. Then the servant prostrated himself before
him, saying, "Have patience with me, and I will pay
you everything." And his master had pity on him,
released him, and forgave him the debt.

But, when he had gone out, that servant found one
of his fellow servants, who owed him a hundred
denaria. And taking him by the throat he said, "Pay
me what you owe me!" And the fellow servant prostrated himself and begged him, saying, "Have patience
with me, and I will pay you." But he refused; and
went and had him put in prison, until he should pay
the debt.

Then his fellow servants, when they saw this, were
greatly offended; and they went and told their master
all that had happened.

Then his master summoned that servant and said:
"You wicked servant! I forgave you all that debt when
you asked me! Ought you not to have had pity on your
fellow servant as I had pity on you?" And his angry
master delivered him to the jailers until he should pay
all that was owing to him.

LOVE OF MONEY

22 Take heed and beware of covetousness!
No man's life is preserved by his riches.

23 Give to him who asks you,
And turn not away from him who seeks to borrow from
           you.

24 No man can serve two masters;
    Either he will hate the one and love the other,
    Or he will hold to the one and despise the other:
You cannot serve God and money.

25 Lay not up for yourselves treasures on earth,
    Where moth and rust corrupt,
    And thieves break through and steal.
But lay up for yourselves treasures in heaven,
    Where neither moth nor rust corrupt,
    And where thieves do not break through and steal.
For where your treasure is,
There will your heart be also.

26   When you give a dinner or a supper, do not invite your friends or your brothers or your relatives or your rich neighbors. For they may return your invitation, and so you will be repaid.

    But when you give a feast, invite the poor, the maimed, the lame, the blind. And you shall be blessed, for they cannot repay you and so you shall be repaid at the resurrection of the righteous.

27   A certain rich man's lands yielded great crops. And he said to himself, "What shall I do? I have no room to store such a yield!" And he decided, "I will do this: I will tear down my barns and build bigger ones, and I will store all my grain and other crops in them; and I will say to myself, 'Man, you have plenty of good things stored up for many years; rest, eat, drink and enjoy yourself'."

    But God said to him, "Fool! This very night you shall die! Then who shall have those things that you have prepared?"

28 In the Temple Jesus was watching how people put money into the treasury. And there came a poor widow, who put in two mites (which make a farthing). And Jesus said,

This poor widow has put in more than all the others!

For they all put in what they did not need; but she has
put in all she had to live on.

UNTRUTH

29 You have heard that it was said,
  "Thou shalt not swear falsely but shalt perform to
        the Lord what thou hast sworn."
But I say to you,
  Take no oath at all:
    Neither by the sky,
      For that is *God's throne;*
    Nor by the earth,
      For that is *the footstool of His feet;*
    Nor by Jerusalem,
      For that is *the city of the Great King;*
    Nor by your head,
      For you cannot make one hair white or black.
But let your language be "Yes, yes" or "No, no";
And anything added to these words is from Satan.

30 Whoever swears, "By the Altar!",
  Swears by it and by all things on it.
Whoever swears, "By the Temple!",
  Swears by it and by Him who dwells in it.
Whoever swears, "By Heaven!",
  Swears by God's Throne and by Him who sits thereon.

IMPURITY

31 You have heard that it was said,
  "Thou shalt not commit adultery."
But I say to you,
    Whoever looks after a woman to lust after her,
    Has already committed adultery with her in his heart.

DIVORCE

32 Pharisees asked Jesus, "Is it lawful for a man to put away his
wife?" And he answered, "What did Moses command you?" And

they said, "Moses gave permission to write a certificate of divorce, and to put her away." But Jesus answered,

Because of the hardness of your hearts he wrote this law. But at the beginning of creation God said, *"Male and female created He them,"* and *"Therefore a man shall leave his father and his mother and shall cleave to his wife: and they twain shall be one flesh."* So they are no longer two; but are one flesh.

What therefore God has joined together, let no man put asunder.

SINGLENESS OF PURPOSE

33 The good man from his good treasure brings out what
is good,
And the evil man from his evil treasure brings out
what is evil;
For from what fills the heart,
The mouth speaks.

34 Every tree is known by its fruits!
Do men gather grapes from thorns?
Or figs from thistles?
Just so every good tree brings forth good fruit,
But the corrupt tree brings forth evil fruit;
A good tree cannot bring forth evil fruit,
Nor can a corrupt tree bring forth good fruit.

35 The light of the body is the eye!
So if your eye is healthy,
Your whole body is full of light;
But if your eye is diseased,
Your whole body is full of darkness.
If the light within you is darkness,
How great is that darkness!

36 The Kingdom of God is like a treasure hidden in a
field; which a man found and hid again, and then joy-

fully went and sold all that he had, and bought that field.

37   Again, the Kingdom of God is like a merchant in search of pearls; who having found one pearl of great price, went and sold all that he had, and bought it.

38 Enter in by the narrow gate!
For wide is the gate and broad the way that leads to destruction,
    And many there are who are entering it;
For narrow is the gate and strait the way that leads to life,
    And few there are who are finding it.

39 It is easier for a camel to go through the eye of a needle
Than for a rich man to enter the Kingdom of God.

40 A man asked Jesus, "Good master, what shall I do to inherit eternal life?" And Jesus answered:
Why do you call me "good"? No one is "good" but God alone!
You know the Commandments: *Thou shalt not kill; Thou shalt not commit adultery; Thou shalt not steal; Thou shalt not bear false witness; Honor thy father and thy mother.*
And he replied, "Master, all these I have kept from my youth." And Jesus, looking at him, loved him and said to him,
You have one lack!
Go; sell all that you have and give it to the poor—and you shall have treasure in heaven—
And come; follow me!
But he went away sorrowful, for he was very rich.

41   A certain rich man had a steward. And he was told that this steward was wasting his property; so he called him and said, "What is this I hear about you? Make up your accounts, for you can be my steward no longer!" And the steward said to himself, "What shall I do, now that my master takes away my stewardship? I am

not strong enough to dig—I am ashamed to beg. I
know what I will do! Then when I am put out of the
stewardship, they will let me live in their houses."

And he called each of his master's debtors. And he
said to the first, "How much do you owe my master?"
And he said, "A hundred measures of oil." And the
steward said to him, "Here is your promise to pay.
Take it; and sit right down and change 'a hundred' to
'fifty'!" Then he said to another, "And how much do
you owe?" And he said, "A hundred measures of
wheat." He said to him, "Take your promise to pay,
and change 'a hundred' to 'eighty'!"

And Jesus praised the cleverness of this dishonest steward, saying,
Worldly men in their affairs,
Are wiser than are the children of light in theirs!

SELF-CONTROL

42 It is impossible but that men will sin,
But woe to the man who is responsible for sin!

43 If your hand causes you to sin, cut it off!
It is better for you to enter into life maimed,
Than having two hands to go into hell.
If your foot causes you to sin, cut it off!
It is better for you to enter into life lame,
Than having two feet to go into hell.
If your eye causes you to sin, pluck it out!
It is better for you to enter into life with one eye,
Than having two eyes to go into hell.

IRRELEVANT MATTERS

44 A certain man said to Jesus, "Master, tell my brother to divide
our inheritance with me." But Jesus answered,
Man, who appointed me a judge or a divider over you?

45 Certain Herodians came to him, to entrap him in his words;
saying, "Master, we know that you always tell the truth and are
afraid of nobody; for you care not how powerful any man seems

to be, but you teach God's way truthfully. Tell us then: Is it in accord with the Law to pay tribute to Caesar? Or not?" But he, seeing their hypocrisy, said, "Why do you tempt me? Bring me a tribute coin, that I may look at it." And they brought one. And he said, "Whose portrait is this? And whose inscription?" And they answered, "Caesar's." And he said,

Render to Caesar the things that are Caesar's,
And to God the things that are God's.

SUMMARY

46 Blessed are they who endure despite oppression,
> For theirs is the Kingdom of God.
Blessed are they who mourn at unrighteousness,
> For they shall be comforted.
Blessed are the gentle,
> For they shall inherit the Promised Land.
Blessed are they who hunger and thirst after righteousness,
> For they shall be filled.
Blessed are the merciful,
> For they shall obtain mercy.
Blessed are the pure in heart,
> For they shall see God.
Blessed are the peacemakers,
> For they shall be called "Sons of God."
Blessed are they who are persecuted for righteousness' sake,
> For theirs is the Kingdom of God.

The False Way of Righteousness

EMPTY CEREMONIALISM

47 There is nothing that goes into a man from without that can defile him;
The things that come from within, these are they that defile a man.

48 You Pharisees strain out a gnat and swallow a camel!

49 You Pharisees pay tithes of mint, anise and cummin;
But have neglected the weightier matters of the Law:
justice, mercy and honesty:
It is these that you ought to have done!

50 You Pharisees cleanse the outside of the cup and of
the platter,
But the food and drink in them have been bought with
the proceeds of extortion and greed.
Cleanse the contents!
Then the cup and the platter will be clean.

51 A Pharisee wondered that Jesus did not wash before eating. But
Jesus answered,
You Pharisees cleanse your outside, but your inside is
full of covetousness;
Did not He who made your outside, make your inside
also?

EVASIONS

52   You blind guides who say, "Who swears 'By the
Temple!' has not taken a binding oath; but who swears
'By the gold on the Temple!' is bound to fulfill his
vow."
You fools and blind! For which is greater, the gold?
Or the Temple that consecrates the gold?
And, "Who swears 'By the altar!' has not taken a
binding oath; but who swears 'By the gift on the altar!'
is bound to fulfill his vow."
You blind! For which is greater, the gift? Or the
altar that consecrates the gift?

SABBATH HARSHNESS

53 The Sabbath was made for man,
Not man for the Sabbath;
Therefore man is the master of the Sabbath.

54 Jesus asked,
   Is it according to the Law to do good on the Sabbath?

55 Jesus healed on the Sabbath and said,
   Which of you, if he has an ass or an ox fallen into a
pit, will not immediately pull him out on the Sabbath?

56 Jesus' disciples plucked grain on the Sabbath. And the Pharisees
asked, "Why do they do what is not lawful on the Sabbath?"
But Jesus answered,
   Did you never read what David did when he and his
men were hungry? How he entered into God's house;
and ate the showbread, which it is unlawful for anyone
to eat except the priests?

57 (After doing good on the Sabbath) Jesus said,
   Have you never read in the Law how on the Sabbath
the priests in the Temple break the Law but are blame-
less? And, I tell you, in the present case there is something more important than the Temple! But, if you
had understood this text, *I desire mercy and not sacrifice,* you would not have condemned the guiltless.

HEARTLESS CRUELTY

58   You scribes reject God's commandment in order to
keep your own tradition. For Moses said, *"Honor thy
father and thy mother,"* and *"If a man speak evil of his
father or his mother, he shall surely be put to death."*
But you say, "If a man shall say to his father or his
mother, 'The support you might have from me I declare dedicated to God' "—then you no longer permit
him to do anything for his father or his mother.
   So you contradict God's word by your tradition!

THE RESULT

59 You load men with burdens painful to bear,
      But you will not stretch out one of your fingers to
            lighten them.

You have taken away the key to knowledge:
 You have not gone in yourself,
 And those who were trying to go in you have pre-
  vented.

60 You are like hidden graves,
 And the men who walk over them do not know
  what they are.

61 You are like whitewashed sepulchers,
 Beautiful from without,
 But filled with dead men's bones.

62 You cross land and sea to make one convert; and,
when you have converted him, you make him twice as
much a child of hell as yourselves.

63 You build the tombs of the prophets and you say,
"If we had lived in the days of our fathers, we would
not have joined with them in killing the prophets."
 But when you say, "our fathers," you admit that you
are their "children"!

64 The scribes love to walk about in long robes, and to be
greeted with deference in public places, to have the
chief seats in the synagogues and the best places at
banquets; yet they devour widows' houses and cloak
their covetousness with long prayers.
 They shall receive the greater condemnation!

65 I tell you truly, the publicans and the harlots go into
 the Kingdom of God before you!

EVIL INFLUENCE

66 If the blind lead the blind,
 Both shall fall into the ditch.

67 Beware of the leaven of the Pharisees!

68 Unless your righteousness exceed that of the scribes

and Pharisees, you shall in no wise enter into the
Kingdom of God.

69 Beware of false prophets,
    Who come to you in sheeps' clothing
    But inwardly are ravening wolves.
By their fruits you shall know them:
    Do men gather grapes from thorns?
    Or figs from thistles?
Just so every good tree brings forth good fruit,
    But the corrupt tree brings forth evil fruit;
A good tree cannot bring forth evil fruit,
    Nor can a corrupt tree bring forth good fruit;
Therefore by their fruits you shall know them.

Man's Choice

THE WARNING

70 Repent; for the Kingdom of God is at hand!

71 What good will it do a man, if he gains the whole
        world but loses his life?

72   When your enemy has had you arrested and is having you brought before the magistrate, use every means
to satisfy him before you come into court. Otherwise
he will bring you before the judge, and the judge will
deliver you to the officer, and the officer will put you
in prison. I tell you, you will not be released until
you pay the very last penny!

73 When you see a cloud rise in the west, you say at once,
    "Rain is coming," and so it does;
And when you see the south wind blow, you say at once,
    "Hot weather is coming," and so it does.
You hypocrites! You predict from the appearance of
    the earth and of the sky;
How is it that you do not predict what the present
    time must bring after it?

74 Jesus was told about those Galileans whose blood Pilate had mingled with their sacrifices. And he said,

Do you think that these Galileans were greater sinners than all the Galileans because these things happened to them?

I tell you, no; but unless you repent, you shall all perish like them!

Or those eighteen men, on whom the tower in Siloam fell and killed them, do you think that they were greater sinners than all the Jerusalemites?

I tell you, no; but unless you repent, you shall all perish like them.

75 There was a certain rich man, who dressed in purple and fine linen, and had luxurious food every day. And a certain beggar, named Lazarus, was placed at his gate, full of sores; he longed to be fed with the crumbs that fell from the rich man's table but, instead, dogs came up to him and licked his sores.

And in time the beggar died; and he was carried away by the angels to the place at the right hand of Abraham. And the rich man also died, and was buried. And in the lower world he looked up, being in torments, and he saw Abraham far off and Lazarus at his right hand. And he cried, saying, "Father Abraham, have pity on me; and send Lazarus that he may dip the tip of his finger in water and cool my tongue, for I am in anguish in this flame." But Abraham said, "Son, remember that you in your lifetime received your good things and Lazarus evil things; but now he is comforted here, but you are in anguish. And, beside that, between us and you there is a great gulf fixed; so that they wishing to cross from here to you cannot, nor may they cross from there to us."

And he said, "I beg you, father, send him to my father's house; for I have five brothers; that he may tell them the truth, so that they too may not come into this place of torment." But Abraham said, "They have Moses and the Prophets; let them hear them." And he said, "No, father Abraham; but if one should go to them from the dead they will repent!" And he said to him, "If they do not hear Moses and the Prophets, neither will they be persuaded though one rose from the dead."

RESPONSIBILITY

76 He who has ears to hear, let him hear!

77 Why do you call me, "Lord! Lord!" but do not do the
    things that I say?

78 The servant who knew his master's will and did not
        do it,
    Shall be beaten with many stripes;
    But the servant who did not know it and did things
        deserving stripes,
    Shall be beaten with few stripes.

79 To whom much is given,
        From him will much be required;
    To whom men have committed much,
        From him will they ask the more.

80 He who is faithful in little,
        Is faithful also in much;
    And he who is unfaithful in little,
        Is unfaithful also in much.

81 To him who has shall be given,
    But from him who has not even what he has shall be
        taken away.

82   A certain man, about to go into another country,
    called his servants and entrusted his property to them;
    to one he gave five talents, to another two, to another

one, to each according to his ability. And he went on his journey.

Then the one who received the five talents went and traded with them, and made five talents more. And in the same way the one who received the two talents made two talents more. But the one who received the one talent went and dug in the ground, and buried his master's money.

Now, after a long time, the master of those servants returned and held an accounting with them. And the one who received the five talents came and said, "Master, you gave me five talents; look, I have made five talents more." And his master said to him, "Well done, good and faithful servant; you have been faithful over a few things, I will set you over many things." And the one, too, who had received the two talents said, "Master, you gave me two talents; look, I have made two talents more." And his master said to him, "Well done, good and faithful servant; you have been faithful over a few things, I will set you over many things."

But the one who received the one talent came and said, "Master, I knew that you are a hard man, reaping what others have sowed and gathering what others have winnowed. So I was afraid; and I went and hid your talent in the ground. And, look, here you have what belongs to you." And his master said, "You wicked and lazy servant! Yet you 'knew' I was a hard man, reaping what others have sowed and gathering what others have winnowed! Then you ought to have put my money in the bank; so that on my return I might have had what belongs to me with interest."

83   When an unclean spirit has gone out of a man, it roams through waterless places, seeking rest. And, finding none, it says, "I will go back to my home that I left." And when it goes back, it finds the house empty, swept and made inviting. So it goes and takes seven other

spirits more wicked than it is; and they go in and live there. So the final condition of that man is worse than it was before!

UNCEASING EFFORT

84 Watch; for you do not know the day or the hour.

85 If the master of the house had known at what hour the thief would come, he would have watched and would not have let his house be broken into.

86 The Kingdom of God is like ten young girls, who took their lamps and went out to meet the bridegroom and the bride. And five of them were wise and five were foolish; for the foolish ones did not take oil with them, when they took their lamps, but the wise ones took oil in vessels along with their lamps. And when the bridegroom's coming was delayed, they all went to sleep.

But at midnight a cry was raised, "Here comes the bridegroom; go and meet him." Then those girls all woke up and trimmed their lamps. And the foolish ones said to the wise ones, "Give us some of your oil, for our lamps are going out." But the wise ones answered, "Not at all; there is not enough for us all; go to the oil-sellers and buy your own oil." And while they were gone to buy, the bridegroom arrived and the girls who were ready went in with him to the marriage supper. And the doors were shut.

Later on the other girls arrived, and cried, "Sir! Sir! Open the door to us!" But he answered, "I don't know you."

SUMMARY

87 Every one who hears these words of mine and does them
Shall be likened to a wise man,

Who built his house on a rock;
And the rains descended,
And the floods came,
And the winds blew,
And beat upon that house,
And it did not fall, for it was built on the rock.
But every one who hears these words of mine and does
them not
Shall be likened to a foolish man,
Who built his house on the sand;
And the rains descended,
And the floods came,
And the winds blew,
And beat upon that house,
And it fell—and great was its fall!

II

THE FATHER

The Father's Call

THE RIGHT AND THE WRONG RESPONSE

88 When little children were brought to Jesus for his blessing, the disciples rebuked those who brought them. But Jesus was indignant and said,

Suffer the little children to come to me and forbid them not, for to such the Kingdom of God belongs.

Whoever shall not receive the Kingdom of God as a little child, shall not enter into it.

89 Two men went up into the Temple to pray; one a Pharisee and the other a publican. The Pharisee stood and prayed thus to himself,

God, I thank thee that I am not as other men are; extortioners, dishonest, adulterers or even like this publican. I fast twice every week; I give tithes of everything that I get.

But the publican, standing a long way off, would not so much as lift up his eyes to heaven, but struck his breast, saying,

God, be merciful to me a sinner.

I tell you, this man went home forgiven rather than the other!

90 Jesus said to the Pharisees,

A certain man had two sons. And he came to the first and said, "My son, go and work today in the vineyard." And he answered, "I will not;" but afterward he was sorry and went.

And he came to the second and said the same. And he answered, "I will go, sir;" but he did not go.

Which of these two obeyed his father?

32

The Pharisees answered, "The first." And Jesus said to them,
I tell you truly; the publicans and the harlots go into
the Kingdom of God before you!

91   The Kingdom of God is like a man who was a householder, who went out early in the morning to hire
laborers for his vineyard. And when he had agreed
with them for a denarion a day, he sent them into his
vineyard. And he went out about nine o'clock and saw
others standing idle in the market place; and he said
to them, "Go into the vineyard too, and I will pay you
whatever is right." And they went to work. Again he
went out about noon and about three o'clock and did
the same. And at about five o'clock he went out and
found others standing, and he said to them, "Why do
you stand here all the day idle?" They answered, "Because no one has hired us." He said, "You, too, may
go into the vineyard."

When evening came, the owner of the vineyard said
to his manager, "Call the laborers and pay them their
wages; but begin with the latest comers and finish with
those who came first." And when those men came
who were hired about five o'clock, each of them received a denarion. And when those first hired came,
they expected to receive more; but they, too, each received a denarion. And when they received it, they
grumbled at the householder, saying, "These late
comers only worked an hour! And you have treated
them as well as us, who have endured the heavy work
of the day and the scorching heat!" But he replied to
one of them, "Friend, I am doing you no injustice!
Did you not agree with me for a denarion? Take what
belongs to you, and go; I have decided to give these late
comers the same as you. Have I not a right to do as I
please with my own money? Or are you envious because I am generous?"

EXAMPLES OF ACCEPTANCE

92 Jesus said to Levi, who was a publican,

Follow me!

And he followed him.

93 Jesus ate and drank with publicans and sinners. And when asked about it, he said,

They who are well have no need of a physician; only they who are sick.

94 A chief publican, named Zacchaeus, because of a crowd about Jesus climbed a sycamore tree to see him. And Jesus looked up and said to him, "Zacchaeus, come down quickly, for I am going to stay at your house today." So he hurried down and welcomed him joyfully. But the people murmured, "He has gone to stay with a man who is a sinner." But Zacchaeus said to Jesus, "Look, sir, I am going to give half of my property to the poor; and if I have cheated anyone of anything, I will pay him back four times as much." And Jesus said,

Today salvation has come to this house.

95 Jesus was eating in the house of a Pharisee. And a woman of that city, who was a sinner, learning that Jesus was there, stood behind him at his feet, weeping; and when she let her tears fall on his feet, she wiped them off with her hair; and she kissed his feet. Now when the Pharisee who had invited Jesus saw it, he said to himself, "If this man were a prophet, he would have known who and what sort of a woman this is who touches him." And Jesus said, "Simon, I have something to say to you." And he answered, "Say on, Master!" And Jesus said,

A certain creditor had two debtors; one owed him five hundred denaria, the other fifty. And when they could not pay, he freely canceled both debts. Which of the two, then, will love him the more?

Simon replied, "I suppose, the one to whom he forgave the more." And Jesus said, "Your answer is right."

THE WELCOME

96   What man among you, who has a hundred sheep and has lost one of them, does not leave the ninety-nine and go after the lost sheep until he finds it? And when he

has found it, he lays it on his shoulders, rejoicing. And when he comes home, he calls together his friends and neighbors, saying, "Rejoice with me, for I have found my sheep that was lost!"

Just so, I tell you, God rejoices over one sinner who repents!

97 What woman, who has ten silver coins and has lost one of them, does not light a lamp and sweep the house and seek with all her might until she finds it? And when she has found it, she calls together her friends and neighbors, saying, "Rejoice with me, for I have found the coin that was lost!"

Just so, I tell you, God rejoices over one sinner who repents!

98 A certain man had two sons. And the younger of them said to his father, "Father, give me now the portion of your estate that I shall inherit." So he divided his estate between the two. And, not many days later, the younger son collected all his property and traveled into a distant country; and there he wasted his substance with riotous living.

And when he had spent all, a great famine arose in that country and he began to be in want. And he went and took service with one of the citizens of that country, who sent him into his fields to tend swine. And he longed to satisfy his hunger with the pods the swine ate; but nobody gave him any. And when he realized his condition, he said, "How many hired servants of my father have food enough and to spare, while I am dying of hunger here! I will arise and go to my father! And I will say to him, 'Father, I have sinned against God and against you; I am no longer fit to be called your son; treat me like one of your hired servants.'"

So he arose and came to his father.

But when he was still a long way off, his father saw him; and he was moved with pity, and ran and embraced him and kissed him. And the son said to him, "Father, I have sinned against God and against you; I am no longer fit to be called your son—" But his father, interrupting him, said to the servants, "Bring quickly the best robe and put it on him, and put a ring on his hand and shoes on his feet. And bring the fatted calf and kill it, and let us eat and celebrate! For this my son was dead and is alive again; he was lost and is found."

So they began to rejoice. Now the elder son was in the field; and as he came and drew near to the house he heard music and dancing. And he called one of the servants, and inquired what this might mean. And he said to him, "Your brother has come; and your father has killed the fatted calf, because he has got him back safe and sound." But he was angry, and refused to go in. And his father came out and entreated him; but he answered, "Look, I have been serving you all these years, and I have never disobeyed any of your orders; and yet you never gave me even a kid to make merry with my friends. But when this son of yours came, who has squandered your property with harlots, you have killed the fatted calf for him!" And he said to him, "My son, you are always with me, and all that is mine is yours. But it was right to make merry and be glad; for this your brother was dead and is alive again; and was lost and is found!"

Life With the Father

SIMPLICITY

99 Take heed that you do not perform your religious acts
    Before men to be seen by them;
For then you will have no reward
    With your Father who is in heaven.

When you give alms,
  Do not trumpet it abroad as the hypocrites do
    In the synagogues and on the street corners, that
        they may be praised by men;
  I tell you truly, they have their reward!
But you, when you give alms,
  Let not your left hand know what your right hand
        does,
    So that your alms may be in secret;
      And your Father, who sees in secret, will re-
        ward you.
When you pray,
  Be not like the hypocrites, who love to pray standing
    In the synagogues and on the street corners, that
        they may be seen by men;
  I tell you truly, they have their reward!
But you, when you pray,
  Go into your room and shut the door,
    And pray to your Father in secret;
      And your Father, who sees in secret, will re-
        ward you.
When you fast,
  Do not try to look wretched as the hypocrites do,
    For they disfigure their faces, that their fasting
        may be noticed by men;
  I tell you truly, they have their reward!
But you, when you fast,
  Make your hair trim and wash your face,
    So that your fasting will not be seen by men, but
        by your Father, in secret;
      And your Father, who sees in secret, will re-
        ward you.

PRAYER

100 When you pray, say,
      Father
        (Hallowed be thy Name!)

May thy Kingdom come.
Give us today our daily bread;
And forgive us our trespasses,
For we forgive those who trespass against us;
And lead us not into temptation.

101 Ask; and it shall be given you;
Seek; and you shall find;
Knock; and it shall be opened to you:
For every one who asks, receives;
And every one who seeks, finds;
And to every one who knocks, it shall be opened.

102 If a son of any of you who is a father asks bread,
Will he give him a stone?
If he asks for a fish,
Will he give him a serpent?
If he asks for an egg,
Will he give him a scorpion?
So, if you, who are evil,
Know how to give good gifts to your children;
How much more will your Father in heaven
Give good things to those who ask Him?

103 When you pray,
Use not empty repetitions as the heathen do;
For they think that they will be heard because
their prayers are long!
So be not like them!
For your Father knows what you need before you
ask Him.

104 If a man should go to a friend at midnight and say,
"Friend, lend me five loaves! A friend of mine who is
on a journey has come to me, and I have no food to
give him," and if he reply from inside the house, "Stop
disturbing me! My door is locked, and my children

are with me in bed; I cannot get up and give you anything,"—still, even though he will not get up and
give him the bread for friendship's sake, yet because of
his persistence he will get up and give him whatever he
needs.

105   There was a judge in a certain city, who neither
feared God nor respected men. And there was a widow
in that city, who came to him, saying, "Give me my
rights!" And for a while he was unwilling. But he
later said to himself, "Even though I neither fear God
nor respect men, yet because of this widow's persistence
I will give her her rights; if I do not, she will keep on
coming and end by assaulting me!"

CONFIDENCE

106 What is impossible to men
    Is possible to God.

107 All things whatever you may ask in prayer, if you be-
        lieve, you shall receive them.

108 If you have faith as a grain of mustard seed,
    You will say to this mountain,
    "Be rooted up and cast into the sea,"
And it will obey you.

109 Be not anxious about tomorrow,
    Let tomorrow be anxious about itself;
Surely there are troubles enough today!

110 Be not anxious about your life,
    What you will eat, or what you will drink;
Nor about your body,
    What you will put on;
Is there not more to life than food?
    And more to the body than clothing?

Look at the birds of the sky!
>They sow not, nor reap, nor gather into barns,
>And yet God feeds them;
Are you not worth more than they?
Who by worrying can prolong his life a single instant?
And why are you anxious about clothing?
>Look at the flowers of the field, how they grow!
>>They toil not, neither do they spin,
>>>And yet, I tell you, even Solomon in all his glory
>>>was not arrayed like one of these!
Therefore, if God so clothes the grass of the field,
>Which today exists, and tomorrow is cast into the oven,
Shall He not much more clothe you, O you of little faith!
Therefore be not anxious,
>Saying, "What shall we eat?" or "What shall we drink?" or "How shall we get clothing?"
These things are the ideals of the heathen,
>But your Father knows that you need these things;
So seek rather the Kingdom of God,
>And all these things shall be given you in addition.

111 A woman named Martha had Jesus in her house; and she had a sister named Mary, who sat at his feet and listened to his teaching. But Martha was engaged in preparing a great meal, and she said, "Sir, do you not care that my sister has left me to do all the work by myself? Tell her to help me!" But Jesus answered, Martha, Martha, you are burdening yourself in preparing many things, when a few things, or even only one, would be enough! Mary has made a better choice, which shall not be taken away from her.

THE FINAL PROMISE

112 Sadducees, who say there is no resurrection, asked Jesus, "Teacher, Moses wrote for us, *'If a man's brother die, leaving a wife but no child, then the man shall take the wife and raise up children for his brother.'* Well, there were seven brothers. The

first took a wife and died childless; and the second took her and died childless; and the third similarly, and so on. And none of the seven left children. In that 'resurrection,' then, when you say 'men rise again,' of which of these men shall she be the wife? All seven of them had her!"

Jesus answered,

Is not your error that you do not know either the
Scriptures or the power of God?

Human beings in this world marry and are given in marriage. But they who are counted worthy to attain the heavenly world neither marry nor are given in marriage, since they can die no more. For they are sons of God, because they are sons of the resurrection.

But as regards the dead, that they are raised, have you never read in the Book of Moses, in the passage about the Bush, how God spoke to Moses, saying, "*I am the God of Abraham, and the God of Isaac, and the God of Jacob*"?

God is not God of the dead but of the living!

You are greatly in error!

SUMMARY

113 Come to me, all you who are weary and heavy burdened,
    And I will give you rest;
    Take my yoke upon you, and learn from me.
For I am gentle, and my heart is with the lowly,
    And you shall find rest for your souls,
For my yoke is easy, and my burden is light.

III

THE MISSION
The Missionaries

THE CALL

114 The harvest truly is plenteous,
    But the laborers are few;
Pray therefore the Lord of the harvest,
    That He will send forth laborers into His harvest.

115 Jesus said to Peter, Andrew, James and John, who were fishermen,
Follow me!
And they left their fishing and followed him.

116 Jesus said to Levi, a publican,
Follow me!
And he left his employment and followed him.

117 Jesus chose twelve,
    That they might be with him and that he might send
        them forth to preach,
Simon, whom he surnamed Peter, James, the son of Zebedee,
and John, James's brother, and Andrew, and Philip, and Barthol-
omew, and Matthew, and Thomas, and James, the son of Alphaeus,
and Thaddaeus, and Simon, the Canaanaean, and Judas Iscariot,
who also betrayed him.

THE COST TO SELF

118 If any man would be my disciple,
    Let him deny himself;
And so let him follow me.

119 Carry no purse, no wallet, no shoes.

120 A certain man said to Jesus, "Master, I will follow you wherever
you go." But Jesus answered,

The foxes have holes,
　And the birds of the air have nests;
But I, a man,
　Have no place to lay my head!

121 Jesus said to a certain man, "Follow me!" But he said, "Master, let me first go and bury my father." But Jesus answered,
Let the dead bury their dead!
But you, go and preach the Kingdom of God.

122 A man said, "Master, I will follow you; but let me first say farewell to my family." But Jesus answered,
No man who puts his hand to the plow
　And then looks back
Is fit for the Kingdom of God.

123 Jesus said to a rich man,
You have one lack!
Go; sell all that you have and give it to the poor—and
　　　you shall have treasure in heaven—
And come; follow me!
But he went away sorrowful.

124 There are some eunuchs,
　Who were born so;
And there are some eunuchs,
　Who were made so by men;
And there are some eunuchs,
　Who made themselves eunuchs,
　For the sake of the Kingdom of God.

125　Which of you, wishing to build a watchtower in his field, does not sit down first and count up the cost, to make sure he has enough to finish it? Otherwise, when he has laid the foundation and is not able to complete the work, all who see it will begin to jeer at him, saying, "This man began to build and could not finish!"

126   Or what king, as he goes to meet another king in war, will not first sit down and seek advice as to whether with ten thousand troops he can face the king who comes against him with twenty thousand? If he finds he cannot, he sends ambassadors, while the other king is still a long way off, and asks for terms of peace.

HOSTILITY FROM OTHERS

127 The disciple is not above his master,
        Nor the servant above his lord;
    It is enough for the disciple to be like his master,
        And the servant like his lord.
    If they have called the master of the house "Beelzebub,"
        How much more will they give this name to his
            household?

128 Think not that I am come to send peace on the earth,
        I am not come to send peace, but a sword!
    I am come to set
        A man against his father,
        And a daughter against her mother,
        And a daughter-in-law against her mother-in-law;
    And
        A man's foes shall be his own family!

129 He who loves father or mother more than me,
        Is not worthy of me;
    And he who loves son or daughter more than me,
        Is not worthy of me.

130 Men will deliver you up to the courts,
        And they will scourge you in their synagogues,
        And you will be brought before governors and kings,
        To testify to them and to the heathen.

THE RESPONSIBILITY

131 A city set on a hill cannot be hid!

132 What I tell you in darkness,
Speak out in the light;
What you hear in a whisper,
Proclaim on the housetops.

133 There is nothing covered that shall not be revealed,
Or hid that shall not be brought to light.

134 You are the salt of the earth!
But if salt loses its saltness,
With what can it be salted?
It is good for nothing,
Except to be thrown out and trampled under foot
by men.

135 You are the light of the world!
Men do not light a lamp and put it under a bushel;
They put it on a stand,
And it gives light to all in the house.
So let your light shine before men;
That they may see your good works,
And glorify your Father who is in heaven.

136 Fear not them who kill the body but cannot kill the
soul;
But fear Him who can destroy both soul and body in
hell.

137 He who finds his life,
Shall lose it;
And he who loses his life for my sake,
Shall find it.

138 Whoever shall confess me before men,
Him shall the Son of Man confess before the angels
of God;
Whoever shall deny me before men,
He shall be denied before the angels of God.

THE JOY

139   The disciples of John the Baptist and the disciples of the Pharisees were observing a fast. And Jesus was asked, "Why do not your disciples fast?" And he answered,
Can a wedding party fast while the bridegroom is with
     them?
Nobody sews a patch of new cloth on an old garment!
     If he does, the hole is made larger.
Nobody puts new wine into old skins!
     If he does, it will burst the skins,
         And the wine is spilled,
         And the skins are ruined.

140   Blessed are you, when men shall reproach you, and persecute you, and say all manner of evil against you, for my sake,
     Rejoice and be exceeding glad!
For great is your reward in heaven,
     For so persecuted they the prophets who were be-
         fore you.

141   Are not two sparrow sold for a farthing?
     Yet not one of them will die without your Father's
         will;
Therefore, fear not!
     You are of more value than many sparrows,
     The very hairs of your head are all numbered.

142   There is no one who has left house or brothers or sisters or mother or father or children or lands for my sake,
     Who will not receive a hundred-fold now in this
         present life;
Houses and brothers and sisters and mothers and
         fathers and children and lands,
     Even though he suffer persecution.
And in the world to come
     He shall have eternal life.

143 If you are brought before judges, be not anxious how
   or what you shall speak,
   For it shall ᴊe given you in that hour what you
      shall speak.
   For it is not you who speak,
   But the Spirit of your Father that speaks in you.

144   You who have been faithful to me in my trials, I give
you royal authority, even as the Father has given it to
me; so that in my Kingdom you shall eat and drink
at my table, and you shall sit on thrones, judging the
twelve tribes of Israel.

The Preaching

CONCENTRATION

145 Salute no man while you are journeying.

146 Go not into a quarter inhabited by heathen, nor
   enter any city of the Samaritans;
   Go rather to the lost sheep of the house of Israel.

147   Into whatever house you enter, first say, "Peace be
to this house!"   And if a man of peace is there, your
blessing shall rest upon him; if not, you yourself shall
have the profit of it.

148 Remain always in the same house; go not from house
   to house.

149 Eat and drink whatever they offer you; for the laborer
   is worthy of his hire.

DISCRETION

150 I send you out as lambs among wolves;
   Be therefore as wise as serpents,
   And as harmless as doves.

151 Give not that which is holy to dogs,
    And cast not your pearls before swine;
      Lest they trample them under their feet,
And turn and rend you.

152   Every scribe who has been instructed in the Kingdom of God is like a man who is a householder: He brings out of his possessions both new things and old things.

THE HEARERS

153 Wisdom is approved by all who are her children.

154 He who hears you, hears me;
    And he who rejects you, rejects me;
      And he who rejects me, rejects Him who sent me.

155 The sower went out to sow his seed:
    And some fell by the wayside,
      And it was trodden under foot,
        And the birds of the air devoured it.
    And some fell on the rock,
      And as soon as it grew up it withered away,
        Because it had no moisture.
    And some fell among thorns,
      And the thorns grew up with it,
        And choked it.
    And some fell on good ground,
      And it grew,
        And brought forth fruit a hundredfold.

156   The Kingdom of God is like a dragnet, that was cast into the sea and gathered fish of every kind. When it was full, they drew it up on the beach; and they sat down, and gathered the good fish into vessels, but the bad they threw away.

IV

THE REJECTION

WRONG EXPECTATIONS

157 Jesus healed many who were sick. And that night, he arose
before dawn, went out into a deserted place and prayed there.
And his disciples found him and said to him, "Everyone is looking
for you." But he answered,
> Let us go to other villages that I may preach there;
> this is the reason why I came away.

158 Jesus came to Nazareth, where he was brought up, and taught
in the synagogue. And they were astonished and said, "Where
did this man get his wisdom? Is he not the carpenter? The son
of Mary; the brother of James and Joses and Judas and Simon?
And are not his sisters here with us?" But Jesus answered,
> A prophet is not without honor: except in his own
> city, and among his own relatives, and in his own
> house.

159   From the days of John the Baptist until now the
Kingdom of God is being snatched at by violence, and
violent men are trying to grasp it: this has come to
pass because the fulfillment of all the Law and the
Prophets began with John.

160 No man who has drunk old wine immediately desires
new, for he says, "The old is good."

161 John the Baptist sent messengers to Jesus, asking, "Are you the
Coming One, or shall we look for another?" But Jesus answered,
> Go and tell John the things you see and hear:
> *The blind receive their sight,*
> The lame walk,
> The lepers are cleansed,
> The deaf hear,
> The dead are raised up,
> And *the "poor" have good tidings preached to them.*

And blessed is he who does not think me evil!

And as the messengers went away, Jesus said to the people about John,

What did you go out into the wilderness to see?
A reed shaken by the wind?
But what did you go out to see?
A man in costly clothing?
You know, men who wear costly clothing are in
kings' palaces!
But what did you go out to see?
A prophet?
Yes, I tell you; and more than a prophet!
I tell you truly,
Among all those born of women there is none greater
than John the Baptist;
Yet, he who is least in the Kingdom of God is greater
than he!

OBSTINACY

162 A sign from heaven was demanded from Jesus. But he answered,
This is an evil generation!
They seek a sign;
And no sign shall be given them,
Except the sign of Jonah, the prophet.

163 Who is not with me is against me,
And who gathers not with me, scatters.

164 Whoever speaks a word against this son of man,
It shall be forgiven him;
But whoever blasphemes against the Holy Spirit,
It shall not be forgiven him.

165 To what shall I liken the men of this generation? To
what are they like?
They are like children, sitting in the market places
and calling to their playmates, "We played weddings,
and you wouldn't dance! We played funerals, and you
wouldn't cry!"

For John came, neither eating nor drinking,
   And you said, "He has a demon!"
I came, both eating and drinking,
   And you say, "A gluttonous man and a wine-bibber;
       who associates with publicans and sinners!"

166 Some men said, "He casts out demons by Beelzebub, the prince of the demons." But Jesus answered,
Every kingdom divided against itself is brought to desolation,
   And a house divided against itself falls;
If Satan is divided against himself,
   How shall his kingdom stand?
If I by Beelzebub cast out demons,
   By whom do your sons cast them out?
     Therefore they shall be your judges!
But if I by the finger of God cast out demons,
   Then the Kingdom of God is touching you!

167   A certain man had a figtree planted in his garden. And he came looking for fruit on it and found none. And he said to the gardener, "Look, for three years I have been coming and looking for fruit on this tree and find none. Cut it down! Why should it cumber the ground?"

And the gardener replied, "Master, leave it alone for this one more year; I will dig up the earth around it and manure it. Then if it bears fruit, all is well; if not, you shall cut it down."

RUIN

168 They shall come from the east and the west and the north and the south,
   And shall sit down in the Kingdom of God,
But there are many last who shall be first,
   And many first who shall be last.

169 There shall be weeping and gnashing of teeth!
>   When you see Abraham and Isaac and Jacob in the
>   Kingdom of God,
>   And you yourself cast out.

170 The Queen of the South will rise up in the Judgment
>   with this generation and will condemn it:
>   For she came from the uttermost parts of the earth
>   to hear the wisdom of Solomon,
>   And, look, something greater than Solomon is here!
>   The men of Nineveh will rise up in the Judgment with
>   this generation and will condemn it:
>   For they repented at the preaching of Jonah,
>   And, look, something greater than Jonah is here!

171 In any city that you enter where they will not receive
>   you, go out into its streets and say,
>   "Even the dust of your city, that clings to our
>   feet, we wipe off against you! Nevertheless know
>   this: The Kingdom of God is at hand!"
>   I tell you, in the Day of Judgment it shall be more
>   tolerable for Sodom than for that city!

172 Woe to you, Bethsaida! Woe to you, Chorazin!
>   If the mighty works had been done in Tyre and
>   Sidon that have been done in you,
>   They long ago would have repented in sackcloth
>   and ashes.
>   So in the Judgment it shall be more tolerable for Tyre
>   and Sidon than for you!

173 You, Capernaum, shall you be exalted in heaven?
>   You shall be cast down to hell!
>   If the mighty works had been done in Sodom that
>   have been done in you,
>   It would have remained to this day.
>   So, I tell you, in the Judgment it shall be more tolerable
>   for the land of Sodom than for you.

174   A certain man made a great supper and invited many. And, at the time set he sent his servant to say to them that had been invited, "Come, for everything is now ready."

And they all with one accord began to make excuses. The first said to the servant, "I have bought a field, and I must go and see it; I beg you, have me excused." And another said, "I have bought five yoke of oxen, and I am going to try them out; I beg you, have me excused." And another said, "I have just got married, and so I cannot come."

And the servant came and told his master all these things.   Then the master of the house grew angry, and said to his servant, "Go out quickly into the streets and lanes of the city; and bring in here the poor and the crippled and the blind and the lame, so that my house may be filled!"

175   A certain man planted a vineyard.   And he set a hedge around it, and dug a pit for the wine vat, and built a watchtower.   And he rented it out to husbandmen and went away into a distant country.   And when the time came, he sent a servant to the husbandmen to collect his share of the yield.   But they took him and beat him; and sent him away empty-handed.   And he sent them another servant, whom they stoned and wounded; and they sent him away shamefully mishandled.   And he sent them yet another; and him they killed.

What, then, will the owner of the vineyard do?

He will come and destroy those husbandmen:

And will give the vineyard to others.

CONVERSION

THE CONVERTS AND THEIR TREATMENT

176 He who receives you, receives me.

177 Whoever does the will of God,
He is my brother and my sister and my mother.

178 He who receives a prophet, because he is a prophet,
Shall receive a reward like the prophet's;
And he who receives a righteous man, because he is a
righteous man,
Shall receive a reward like the righteous man's;
And he who gives you only a cup of cold water, because
you are my disciples,
I tell you truly, he shall not lose his reward.

179 Jesus took a child, embraced it, and said to his disciples,
Whoever receives one such child in my name, re-
ceives me;
And whoever receives me, receives Him who sent me.

180　Whoever drives away one of these little ones, it were
better for him if a great millstone were hanged around
his neck and he were plunged into the depth of the sea.

181 A disciple said to Jesus, "Master, we saw a man casting out
demons in your name; and we forbade him, for he would not
follow us." But Jesus answered,
Do not forbid him!
No one can do a sign in my name, and then quickly
speak against me.

182 Jesus said to his disciples,
The kings of the heathen lord it over them,
And their great ones claim power over them;
It is not so among you!

Whoever wishes to be great among you,
Shall be your servant;
And whoever wishes to be first among you,
Shall be your slave.

183 How does a servant prove himself faithful and wise,
when his master has put him in charge of the other
servants, to give them their food at the proper times?
Happy is such a one if his master, when he comes, finds
him doing as he was commanded: I tell you truly, he
will promote him to the charge of all his possessions.

But if that servant behaves badly, saying to himself,
"My master will not come for a long time," and begins
to beat his fellow servants, and to eat and drink with
drunkards, his master will come on a day when he does
not expect him and at an hour that he does not know;
and he will have him terribly flogged and will put him
with the dishonest slaves.

FAITH AMONG THE HEATHEN

184 A heathen woman, of Syrophoenician race, came to Jesus and
asked him to cast a demon out of her daughter. But he answered,
It is not right to take the children's bread, and to
throw it to the housedogs.
But she replied, "True; yet the dogs under the table eat the
children's leavings." And Jesus answered,
Because of this answer the demon has gone out of
your daughter.

185 In Capernaum a centurion came to Jesus, imploring him and saying, "My servant in my house is paralyzed and in great pain."
Jesus replied, "Do you expect me to come and heal him?" The
centurion answered, "Sir, I am not worthy that you should come
under my roof! Just speak a word, and my servant will be cured.
For I know what authority is! I am under it myself; and I have
soldiers under me: I say to this man, 'Go,' and he goes; and to
another, 'Come,' and he comes; and to my servant, 'Do this,' and
he does it." And Jesus said,
I have not found such faith in all Israel.

THE PRESENT KINGDOM

186 Blessed are the eyes which see the things that you see!
     For, I tell you, many prophets and kings
     Desired to see the things which you see,
        And saw them not;
     And to hear the things which you hear,
        And heard them not.

187 If I by the finger of God cast out demons,
     Then the Kingdom of God is touching you.

188 If a strong man armed guards his house,
     His goods are in peace;
     But if a man stronger than he attack him and over-
        come him,
     He takes from him the arms in which he trusted,
     And seizes the goods for his own.

189 Jesus sent out his disciples to preach and to heal. And they re-
turned with joy, saying, "Lord, even the demons are subject to us
in your name!" And he said,
I was watching Satan fall like lightning from heaven!
Look, I have given you authority to tread upon serpents
        and scorpions,
Authority over all the power of the Enemy;
And nothing shall ever hurt you.
None the less, do not rejoice because the spirits are
        subject to you;
Rejoice because your names are written in heaven!

190 In that very hour Jesus rejoiced and said,
     I thank thee, Father, Lord of heaven and earth,
        That thou didst hide these things from the wise
            and prudent,
        And didst reveal them to babes;
     This, Father, is right, for such was thy good pleasure.
     All things have been revealed to me by the Father!
        And no one knows who the Son is, except the Father,
        And he to whom the Son reveals it.

191 Among all those born of women, there is none greater
        than John the Baptist;
    Yet, he who is least in the Kingdom of God is greater
        than he.

192   So is the Kingdom of God, as when a man sows seed
    in the ground.   Then he sleeps and wakes, night and
    day; and the seed springs up, although he knows not
    how.   The earth bears fruit of herself: first the blade;
    then the ear; then the full corn in the ear.

193 To what shall I liken the Kingdom of God?
        It is like a tiny grain of mustard seed, which a man
    took and planted in his garden.   And it grew and be-
    came a tree; and the birds made their home in its
    branches.

194 To what shall I liken the Kingdom of God?
        It is like leaven, which a woman took and kneaded
    into three great measures of meal.   And it leavened
    them all.

THE MESSIAH

195 In the region of Caesarea Philippi Jesus asked his disciples, "Who
    do men say that I am?"   And they answered, "John the Baptist;
    but some say, 'Elijah,' and others, 'One of the prophets.'"   And
    he said, "But who do you say that I am?"   And Peter answered,
    "The Messiah."   And he charged them not to reveal this to anyone,
    and he began to teach them that he must suffer many things.   And
    Peter started to rebuke him.   But, looking at all his disciples, he
    said to Peter,
    Get thee behind me, Satan!
    Your thoughts are the thoughts of men:
    Not the thoughts of God.

196 I came to cast fire on the earth;
        How great is my longing to know it is kindled!
    I must pass through dark waters;
        How great is my trouble until this is accomplished!

197 Jesus was told, "Leave Herod's country, for he is planning to kill
you." But he answered,
Go and tell that fox,
"Look, I shall go on casting out demons and work-
ing cures today and tomorrow, while on the third
day I shall achieve my destiny."
Nevertheless, by those three days I shall be out of
Herod's country,
For no prophet should die outside of Jerusalem!

198 James and John said to Jesus, "Grant that one of us may sit on
your right hand and the other on your left hand in your glory!"
But Jesus answered,
You know not what you ask!
Can you drink the cup that I must drink?
And pass through the waters through which I must pass?
They replied, "We can!" But Jesus said,
You shall truly drink the cup that I must drink,
And pass through the waters through which I must
pass;
But to sit on my right or on my left is not mine to grant,
But is reserved for those for whom it is prepared.

199 When they were close to Jerusalem, Jesus said to two of his disciples, "Bring me an ass's colt from the village." And they brought
it and spread their garments over it, and Jesus mounted it. And
many spread their garments in the road, and others green branches,
which they cut from the trees. And they who went before him and
they who followed cried,
Hosanna! Blessed be he who cometh in the name of the Lord!
Blessed be the coming Kingdom of our father David! Hosanna
in the highest!

200 Jesus went into the Temple; and he drove out all who sold and
bought in it, and he overthrew the tables of the money-changers
and the seats of those who sold the doves. And he said,
It is written,
My House shall be called a House of prayer;
But you have made it *a den of thieves!*

201 Rulers of the Jews came to Jesus in the Temple and demanded:
"By what authority do you do these things? And who gave you
the authority to do them?" Jesus replied, "I will ask you one

question; answer it, and I will tell you my authority: The baptism of John, was it from heaven or from men?" They answered, "We cannot tell." And Jesus said,

Nor will I tell you my authority!

202 How can the scribes say that the Messiah is David's "son"?

David himself, inspired by the holy Spirit, said:

God said to my Lord,
Sit thou on my right hand,
Until I make thine enemies thy footstool.

David himself calls him "Lord"!
So how can he be his "son"?

203 A woman poured costly ointment on Jesus' head. And those who saw it complained, "Why this waste? This ointment might have been sold at a high price, and the money given to the poor." But Jesus answered,

She has wrought a good work on me!

You have the poor always with you,

And whenever you wish you can do them good;

But me you do not have always with you.

204 At the last supper Jesus said,

I have ardently longed to eat this passover with you; for, I tell you: I shall not eat it again until the passover shall be fulfilled in the Kingdom of God.

And taking a cup, he pronounced the thanksgiving and then he said,

Take this and share it among yourselves; for, I tell you: From henceforth I shall not drink the fruit of the vine until that day when I drink it new in the Kingdom of God.

205 And taking bread, he pronounced the thanksgiving and then he broke it and gave to them. And he said,

Take it; this is my body.

And taking the cup, he pronounced the thanksgiving and gave it to them, and they all drank from it. And he said,

This is my *"blood of the Covenant,"* which is shed for many.

206 One of you, who dips with me in the dish, shall be-
       tray me!

   For the son of man goes,

   Even as the Prophets have written;

   But woe to that man, through whom he is betrayed!

   It were better for that man if he had not been born!

207 Peter said, "Lord, I am ready to go with you to both prison and to
death." But Jesus answered,

   I tell you, this very night, before the second cock-
       crow, you will deny me three times.

208 Jesus said to his disciples, "When I sent you out, without purse
and wallet and shoes, did you lack anything?" They answered,
"Nothing!" And he said,

   But now: he who has a purse, let him take it and like-
       wise a wallet;

   And he who has no sword, let him sell his cloak and
       buy one.

209 And they went to a place called Gethsemane. And he took Peter
and James and John, and said, "My heart is sad to the breaking
point; stay here and keep awake." And he went on a little way,
fell to the ground, and prayed,

   Father; all things are possible to thee;

   Take away this cup!

   Yet not what I will,

   But what thou willest.

     And coming back, he found the three asleep. And he said,
"Simon, are you asleep? Could you not keep awake a single hour?
Wake up, all of you; and pray that you may not fail in the coming
trial!"

   Your hearts are willing, I know,

   But human nature is weak.

210 When the court had assembled to try Jesus, the high priest asked
him, "Are you the Messiah, the Son of the Blessed one?" And
Jesus answered,

   I am!

   And you shall see

The Son of Man sitting on the right hand of the Power,
And
Coming on the clouds of heaven!

THE CONSUMMATION

211 In Jerusalem, a disciple looking at the Temple said, "Master, what splendid stones! What splendid buildings!" But Jesus answered,
Do you see these great buildings?
There shall not be left one stone upon another that
shall not be cast down!

212 Being asked when the Kingdom of God would come, he said,
The coming of the Kingdom cannot be computed;
Nor will men say, "Look, here it comes!" or, "Look,
there it comes!"
For the Kingdom of God will be in your midst!

213 As the lightning comes from the east and shines across
to the west,
So shall be the coming of the Son of Man.

214 This generation shall not pass away until all these
things are fulfilled:

215 But the day and the hour no man knows;
No, not the angels of God;
Not even the Son;
Only the Father.

216 Days will come when you will long to see one of those
days of the Son of Man;
With a longing that is in vain.

217 Take the figtree as a parable:
When its branches become soft with sap and it begins to put forth leaves, you know that summer is
near;
Just so, when you see these things happening, know
that the end is at the door.

218   As it was in the days of Noah,
      So shall it be in the days of the Son of **Man:**
        They were eating,
        They were drinking,
        They were marrying,
        They were being given in marriage,
      Until the day that Noah entered the ark,
And the flood came and destroyed them all.

As it was in the days of Lot,
      So shall it be in the days of the **Son of Man:**
        They were buying,
        They were selling,
        They were planting,
        They were building,
      Until the day that Lot went out of Sodom,
And fire rained from heaven and destroyed them **all.**

219   Two men shall be working in the same field,
      One shall be taken and the other left;
Two women shall be grinding at the same mill,
      One shall be taken and the other left;
Two shall be on the same bed,
      One shall be taken and the other left.

220   Wherever the carcase is,
There will the vultures be gathered together!

221   When the Son of Man shall come in his glory and all the angels with him, then shall he sit on the throne of his glory and shall gather all the nations before him. And he shall separate them from one another before him, as a shepherd separates the sheep from the goats. And he shall set the sheep on his right hand, but the goats on his left hand.
Then shall the King say to those on his right hand: Come, ye blessed of my Father,
Inherit the Kingdom prepared for you from the foundation of the world.

For I was hungry, and you gave me meat;
Thirsty, and you gave me drink;
I was a stranger, and you took me in;
Naked, and you clothed me;
Sick, and you visited me;
In prison, and you came to me.

Then shall the righteous answer him, saying, "Lord, when saw we thee hungry and fed thee, or thirsty and we gave thee drink? When saw we thee a stranger and took thee in, or naked and clothed thee? And when saw we thee sick or in prison and came to thee?"
And the King shall answer them,
I tell you truly: Inasmuch as you did it to the least of these my brethren, you did it to me!

Then shall he say to those on his left hand:
Depart from me, ye cursed,
Into the eternal fire prepared for the devil and his angels.

For I was hungry and you gave me no meat;
Thirsty, and you gave me no drink;
I was a stranger, and you took me not in;
Naked, and you clothed me not;
Sick and in prison, and you visited me not.

Then shall they answer him, saying, "Lord, when saw we thee hungry, or thirsty, or a stranger, or naked, or sick, or in prison and did not minister to thee?"
Then shall he answer them, saying,
I tell you truly: Inasmuch as you did not do it to the least of these, you did not do it to me.
And these shall depart into eternal punishment; but the righteous into eternal life.

COMMENTARY

THE PREPARATION

FOR nearly two hundred years before Jesus' ministry until almost a hundred years afterward (that is, from about 165 B. C. to 135 A. D.) the Jews were expecting the immediate fulfillment of the promises of God made in the Old Testament. During many centuries they had lived under the rule of foreigners: the rule of the Assyrians; the rule of the Babylonians; the rule of the Persians; the rule of the Greeks; the rule of the Romans. Now they hoped soon to live under the rule of God alone.

The coming age in which this rule would be established they called "The Kingdom of God." But they recognized this age could never come by human means; for this the Jews were too weak and their enemies too strong. Moreover, the present world seemed to them to be so utterly evil that it was past reformation; God, they thought, must destroy it altogether. Then He would hold the Last Judgment and drive away all evil men; then at last the Kingdom would come, in which the righteous would dwell in everlasting joy.

This belief, taught to every Jewish school-child, was held by almost every Jew in Palestine; and hardly anyone thought of the future differently. It was in these terms that John the Baptist delivered his message, for no other language would be understood or accepted than the "adventist" terms depicting the end of the world. Preachers everywhere were proclaiming that the Kingdom of God was at hand and that men must repent, for God's Judgment would quickly come; if men did not turn from their sins, they would receive eternal condemnation.

What was new in the Baptist's message was his accusation of his countrymen. Only too many Jews thought that they were safe because they belonged to the Chosen People;

that God would pardon in them what He condemned in
others.   This easygoing confidence the Baptist shattered.
However pure might be their Hebrew ancestry, their moral
conduct would be all that mattered; of what use would be
the claim to be "children of Abraham" by men who were
behaving like "children of vipers"? If God needed children
of Abraham, He could create them out of stones!   It was
as if a woodcutter had come out to a forest and had laid
down his ax for a moment while he made his choice; soon
every useless tree would be cut down and burned.

In the Baptist's day, when a non-Jew became a Jew, he
was "baptized," immersed in water to remove the defilement
of his past life; a ceremony derived from the washings of
unclean persons directed by the Old Testament (Leviticus
15: 5, etc.).   Now the Baptist demanded a new thing: that
Jews should humble themselves, and acknowledge that they
needed cleansing just as much as the "heathen" did.   If
their repentance was sincere, God would forgive them; if
not, their fate was hopeless.   For a Mightier One was approaching, holding—so to speak—in one hand holy Spirit
for the righteous, but in the other hand fire for the wicked.

With a change of figure the Baptist describes the approaching crisis in terms of the "threshing floor," the hard
level space outside Jewish villages on which harvested grain
was poured.   Threshers beat the mass with flails until the
wheat was loosened from the husks ("chaff").   Then the
winnowers came with their "fans"—the older English name
for light shovels—and tossed the mixed wheat and chaff into
the air.   The wind carried the chaff away but the heavier
wheat fell back on the floor, to be gathered into the store-
houses while the useless chaff was burned.   So would it be
in the approaching Judgment!

b

To John's baptism Jesus came.   Not because He was con-
scious of "sin," in our sense of the word, for in His teaching
there is not the faintest trace of any impediment or cloud

in His relation to the Father. But the Baptist's summons was to the whole nation, and as a member of the nation Jesus obeyed the summons. He submitted to the baptism, and as He came up out of the Jordan He had an intense inner experience: a vision as of the heavens opening and the Spirit—in the Old Testament God's gift of power (Numbers 11: 25, etc.)—descending into Him. (Among the Jews the dove appears to have been a symbol of the Spirit; perhaps from Genesis 1: 2 where the Spirit is said to "brood" upon the waters.) And God's voice addressed Him in the threefold title, "Son," "Beloved," "Chosen One." (The usual translation here does not give the sense; "in whom I am well pleased" really means "on whom I have set my choice.") "Son" comes from Psalm 2, "Beloved" and "Chosen One" from Isaiah 42: 1; and all three terms were to the Jews equivalent to the single supreme title "Messiah."

"Messiah" means "Anointed One," from the Old Testament ceremony of anointing with oil to give royal (1 Samuel 16: 13, etc.) or priestly (Exodus 28: 41, etc.) office. But in Jesus' day the title was reserved for the One whom God would appoint to bring the Kingdom. Who this One would be or of what nature he would be was entirely uncertain, and all sorts of opinions were held. At the lowest the Messiah was described as a mere military leader; at the highest as a purely heavenly Being, already seated at God's right hand; and between these extremes all conceivable views were put forth. The single element common to all the definitions was solely that the Messiah must not only proclaim but must actually *bring* the Kingdom.

C

Since there were so many conceptions of Messiahship, it was not enough for Jesus to know that He was Messiah; what *kind* of Messiah had God called Him to be?

To answer this question demanded long meditation in solitude, so He went away into the uninhabited country. So deeply immersed was He in His task that He took no thought of His bodily needs until He felt actual hunger. Then the thought came to Him, "The teachers say that the Messiah can work any miracle; why, then, should I not turn these stones into bread?" But He dismissed the suggestion as from the devil. Always He had regarded every event of His life, whether pleasant or painful, as expressing God's will for Him and therefore to be accepted. Hunger must be satisfied according to the laws God has prescribed (Deuteronomy 8: 3; the traditional "every word that proceedeth out of the mouth of God" is not clear); to attempt to create bread by a miracle that would overthrow all these laws would be rebellion against God. Jesus had powers not possessed by other men. But He used them only in accord with God's whole purpose for the world; never to escape difficulties nor for any other selfish reason. He might have silenced His enemies by a "sign," but when they asked for one, He refused absolutely (§162).

Again the thought came to Him, "Many teachers say that the Messiah will be a great general" (§202); "may I not conquer the world and rule over it?" Again the suggestion was dismissed as from the devil. War can never make men holy; on the contrary, it makes them and their masters brutes, servants of Satan. And man must serve God alone (Deuteronomy 6: 13).

"But am I Messiah at all? There is a way I can prove it! If I jump from the pinnacle of the Temple and am really Messiah, God has promised (Psalm 91: 11-12) that His angels will rescue me; why not put it to the test?" But to attempt this would be to put God to trial. In the ordinary course of life He gives men light enough to see their way; for extraordinary purposes He gives an inner call for guidance. To demand more than this is rebellion (Deuteronomy 6: 16).

By the temptations, then, three things were settled for Jesus. The reality of His call and of His duty must never again be questioned. No appeal must be made to Jewish patriotism, to race-prejudice, or to force. Least of all to the "supernatural" force of a miracle; if men's hearts could not be won by teaching goodness, they could not usefully be won at all (§75). Therefore He began His ministry simply by proclaiming the nature of righteousness as revealed by God.

I

RIGHTEOUSNESS

1

To every Jew God's revelation to man is set forth in the Old Testament; a conviction that Jesus shared absolutely. But how should the Old Testament be understood?

According to the teachers of the time—the "scribes" ("experts in the Law")—the Old Testament was to be treated like a law-book: as a collection of many laws, each binding independently of the others; each to be interpreted strictly according to its exact wording. To Jesus, on the other hand, the Old Testament was a unit, in which a single fundamental principle was to be used in explaining everything else. This principle—quoted from Deuteronomy 6: 4-5—is man's active and complete love of God; if a man gives God his heart and soul and mind and strength, his life must be a Godlike life.

To this "first" commandment a "second" is added (Leviticus 19: 18), which is really not an addition to the "first" but a deduction that must follow from it inevitably (§3); a true love of God brings with it an equally true love of man. And just so a true love of man involves a true love of God.

2

Here Jesus in giving the Golden Rule uses the "second" commandment of §1 to include the "first" as well.

In the Sermon on the Mount the "theme" is stated in Matthew 5: 17 and the "summary" in Matthew 7: 12; by bringing the two together the underlying unity of the Sermon is made clearer. "The Law and the Prophets" is a common phrase for the Old Testament as a whole; here the prophets are named not as predicting the future but as teaching men right conduct. The traditional "fulfill" should be explained as "make their full demands known."

To Jesus goodness must find expression in activity. An earlier Jewish teacher had said, "Whatever is displeasing to thee, do not to thy neighbor," but this ideal is worlds apart from that of Jesus. Christian character is not expressed in refraining from evil but in doing good.

3

The quotation is not from the Old Testament, which contains no such verse. It is quoted from the way the teachers of the day summarized the Law; it was from these that the people "heard" it.

It is a typical lawyers' deduction from Leviticus 19: 18, accented as if it read, "Thou shalt love (only) thy *neighbor* as thyself." So understood, if a man is not a "neighbor" (compare §6) there is no obligation to love him; indeed, if he is an "enemy," there may be a positive obligation to *hate* him. Only too commonly this obligation of hate was applied to the enemies of the Jews, especially the Romans, with the patriotic appeal that every good Jew should detest the enemies of his nation.

Jesus replies that God never so spoke; that this lawyers' summary is contrary to the nature of God, who sends His blessings of sunshine and rain on the good and the evil alike. So if we look on God as Father, it will be our wish to act as He acts. In one sense every human being is a child of God by creation, but unless there is likeness of character between child and father there can be no real sympathy. So it is not enough to *be* a child of God naturally; each person must *become* a child of God morally. And it is the task of so becoming that is the task of righteousness.

To put it differently, in this saying Jesus gives as the deepest principle of conduct the imitation of God.

In this passage and in many others "love" does not mean "emotional feeling" but "unselfish action." Compare the magnificent description of Christian love in 1 Corinthians 13, where everything is centered on what love *does* but not a single word on how love *feels*,

4

Affectionate emotion is not in itself a virtue at all but a purely natural instinct. It is as common among bad men as good and may quite as easily lead to crime as to self-sacrifice. As an example Jesus takes the "publicans." No modern phrase quite gives the force of this term; to the people they figured primarily as "tax collectors," but in the ancient world their legal authority to collect was so poorly safeguarded that dishonesty was only too easy for them; they were looked upon much as are the ward politicians of the present day. These men had family affections; but for that very reason were often more grossly unscrupulous. (Incidentally, it is not true that in Galilee the publicans were hated because they represented the Roman government; they represented the Jewish Tetrarch ["minor king"] Herod Antipas [compare §185]).

Ancient "greetings" usually took the form of a prayer, among Jews " (God's) peace be with thee." It was therefore given only to friends.

The traditional "Ye shall be perfect as your heavenly Father is perfect" is so broad as to command an absolute impossibility for man (§40). The context shows that the meaning is, "Your desire to help others shall be as all-embracing as is the Father's, when He sends His rain on the just and on the unjust."

5

Another form in which Jesus taught the lesson of §4. Note the careful structure: the three terms "love," "do good," and "lend" are first treated separately in parallel form and then are gathered together in the summary.

The Old Testament forbade the Jews to take interest on a loan to one of their own people (Exodus 22: 25, etc.), so that willingness to lend was counted among the virtues (Psalm 112: 5, etc.).

6

Since the teachers ruled that a man was bound to love only his "neighbor" (§3), the question "Who is my neighbor?" was constantly asked. Jesus' story gives the perfect answer: "My neighbor is the man who is near me."

The Samaritans lived just south of the Galilean border. Although Jews of a sort, they had such peculiar customs that they were hated and ridiculed by the other Jews. Yet a Samaritan could prove a better neighbor than a priest or a Levite: the Jewish "clergy."

This story was told by Jesus to explain the meaning of "neighbor" *and for no other reason*. There are no hidden meanings ("allegories") in it: it is an illustration of a truth, not a puzzle; told to help, not to confuse. The event is placed on the way from Jerusalem to Jericho because this road, running through barren country, was notoriously unsafe. The priest and the Levite pass by "on the other side" simply to avoid responsibility. A mixture of oil and wine was a common remedy for wounds, the alcohol in the wine acting as an antiseptic, the oil relieving pain. To ask about the "spiritual meaning" of the inn or anything else in the story is pointless; all the details mean just what they appear to mean and nothing more. This principle is always to be kept in mind in explaining Jesus' stories ("parables").

In the translation "money" is used for the original "two denaria" to avoid distracting the reader's attention by an unimportant detail. A "denarion" (the Latin *denarius*) was a small silver coin, about equal to two American dimes. But the purchasing value of money was very much greater than at present—probably more than ten times as great—so that the actual worth of the two denaria might be something like five dollars.

7-8

All satisfaction with self and contempt for others—the qualities that make "pride"—stand in sharp contrast to the love that Jesus taught. Men who give themselves over to such indulgences will have a terrible awakening when they learn the truth about themselves.

9

When we criticize other people, we set up for them in our mind a moral standard by which we judge them. But we lose all right to ask God to judge us by an easier standard. Compare §§14-21.

10

The "beam" is the unloving spirit that leads us to criticize our neighbors; it is so serious a sin that in comparison many other shortcomings are only "motes" (tiny bits of dust). Faultfinders only make other people worse; if we wish to help a man overcome a bad habit, we must begin with genuine sympathy.

11

Why should we be proud at having done what is right? If a man does nothing else all his life, he has only done his duty.

In the last sentence the traditional "unprofitable" is wrong, for a servant who does his full duty is certainly of value to his master (§§82, 183). "Mere" gives the sense.

12

The quotation is again (§3) a lawyers' summary which the Jews had "heard" from their teachers. It combines the Sixth Commandment (Exodus 20: 13) with some such passage as Exodus 21: 12 so as to bring the crime and the punishment together; modern criminal statutes have the same form, "Whoever willfully and with malice aforethought kills a human being is guilty of murder in the first degree, and on conviction shall suffer the penalty of death." So as a statement of criminal law the teachers' summary was perfectly fair.

But it ought never to have been given as declaring a religious truth; in this sense it was hopelessly inadequate, for it implies that a murderer has nothing worse to fear than the death penalty. Therefore Jesus answers that this penalty is no measure at all of a murderer's guilt in God's sight. God may judge an angry thought as severely as the Jews judged murder; He may judge an abusive word as severely as the Jews judged blasphemy (to them a graver crime than murder); He may judge a vicious curse as severely as the Jews judged atrocious crimes punished by the extreme penalty of burning.

The passage is often taken to mean that Jesus called anger as bad as murder. This is of course untrue. He said that anger in God's eyes may be as bad as murder is in men's eyes; murder, therefore, in God's eyes would be so incomparably worse that no human punishment could begin to measure its guilt.

We do not know the exact meaning of the ancient word "raca" in the traditional versions nor of the word translated "thou fool," but "abuse" and "curse" give the general sense. In the first of the three parallel sentences the traditional "judgment" means the death sentence of a criminal court. In the second sentence "council" means the Great Sanhedrin of Jerusalem, which alone could try cases of blasphemy and other especially grave offenses. In the third sentence "hell of fire" is wholly wrong; in each sentence the second part describes a human, not a divine, punishment: "Valley of Hinnom" is the correct rendering. This valley lies around the southwest corner of Jerusalem. In Old Testament times it had been given over to idolatry (Jeremiah 7: 31, etc.); the Jews therefore deemed it so defiled that they used it as a place of execution for the worst criminals.

In the first sentence after "brother" the Authorized Version adds "without a cause." This is no part of the New Testament but is a well-meant attempt of some later Christian to state an exception: "This does not apply when anger is justified." But anger, in Jesus' sense of a sin against love, can never be justified.

13

This passage deals with what is called a "conflict of duties." It was a duty to offer sacrifice; it was a duty to make good an injury: which duty comes first? Some teachers might have argued that offering sacrifice was a duty to God and making good an injury a duty only to man, so that the former was more important. But in Jesus' teaching making good an injury to a man is just as much a duty to God as offering sacrifice; more so, in fact, for God desires mercy more than sacrifice (§57).

Consequently, Jesus invariably ruled that a "moral" commandment is always weightier than a "ceremonial" commandment (especially §§47-69).

14-15

There can be no "forgiveness" without "forgivingness."

Of course, if by "forgiveness" is meant only the remission of a penalty, God might arbitrarily forgive anyone; when a governor pardons a criminal, the latter is immediately released from prison without regard to his moral character. But God's forgiveness means more than this: it means restoration of the soul to its place as God's child. Not even God can so restore a soul that refuses to part with its hatred.

16

As in §§14-15 Jesus assumes the truth that "it takes two to make forgiveness"; if a person inflicting an injury does not regret it, restoration of true friendship is impossible. Yet, of course, even then the injured person is not freed from his duty of love (§18).

17

The "seven times" of §16 does not mean "only seven times." There is no limitation.

18

In this case the summary the people have heard from their teachers is really found in the Old Testament (Exodus 21: 24). But there it states the law to be followed by judges in a criminal trial, and was never meant as a principle to guide individuals. To protect society criminals must be punished, but this does not justify anyone in demanding revenge. The duty of love is in no way affected by another person's malice, no matter whether expressed in a physical assault or an unjust claim to one's property or labor. (The traditional "compel thee to go one mile" implies "to carry a burden.")

It must not be forgotten, however, that here Jesus is speaking only to the *individual* conscience: "As far as *I* am concerned, this is what *I* should do." He does not say, "If a man smite thy wife, let him smite thy daughter also," or "If a man sue for the widow's bread, let him take the orphans' also," or "If a man force his employees to work twelve hours a day, let him force them to work eighteen." A duty of love is owed to such sufferers even more than to the aggressor!

19

Another form in which Jesus gave the teaching of §§10, 14-18. In the last line "lap" is clearer to modern readers than the traditional "bosom." The latter, however, is the term actually used: in the Orient the "bosom" of the loose outer robe, tightly girded at the waist, is a convenient receptacle for even bulky articles.

20

The disciples remember Elijah's behavior in 2 Kings 1: 10-12.

21

In New Testament times "talent" meant simply "6,000 denaria," so that (§6) the modern purchasing value of

10,000 talents would be well over $100,000,000. This enormous sum is chosen to show the impossibility of any man's paying God the "debt" due Him. "A hundred denaria" might equal $200 or thereabouts: not a trifling sum—the injuries men do to one another are real—but utterly insignificant compared to the other debt. The further details, however, are simply part of the story told as a story; they have no "spiritual" meaning; and attempts, for instance, to identify the "jailers" only lead to confusion.

22

Men come to regard money as the supreme good of life. But they forget what is all-essential, namely, life itself. This money can never guarantee. Compare §27.

23

Another form in which Jesus taught part of the lesson of §18. Here as there the words are addressed to the individual conscience as a warning against selfish grasping. But Jesus does not, of course, mean, "Give the money for your children's bread to the first beggar who asks for it;" the children too are asking for it.

24

The ideal of selfish "success" and the ideal of goodness clash constantly, and no man can hold them both. For a sharper expression of this truth compare §39 and for a concrete example §123.

25

Among the poorer classes in the Orient "treasures" are chiefly fine garments—always in danger of moths—and implements or ornaments of iron or copper—always in danger of rust—while the houses offer little protection against robbery. Very few of Jesus' hearers would have had treasures of gold or strongly-built homes; but even under the best conditions there was—and is today—a constant peril of loss.

Yet men will toil ceaselessly to accumulate wealth—only to see it vanish.

26

Among the poorer classes of Palestine a "dinner" or a "supper" was an extraordinary event, demanding long economy and so usually planned with a shrewd eye to future benefits.

27

The dangers of §25 may be escaped. But there is one danger that cannot be escaped.

The rich man in this story is the perfect example of the folly of selfishness; he thinks only how to enjoy his own life—the very thing that his riches cannot buy for him (§22). Nor would it have made any real difference if God had allowed him to live a little longer, for the end must always be the same.

The answer to the final question is simply "Not you!" The man naturally had heirs, but neither he nor the story is interested in them.

28

In sharpest contrast to the selfish man in §27 is this poor widow, who goes hungry rather than neglect an opportunity to give.

A "mite" was the smallest coin of the ancient world, in purchasing value nearly enough equivalent to an American cent. Writers sometimes assert that Jews were forbidden to put only one mite into the Temple treasury, but this is a mistake; the point is that she might have kept back one of her two coins but gave them both.

29-30

What the people had "heard" from their teachers is here a brief summary of the Third Commandment (Exodus 20: 7). It was objectionable only because of the way (compare §3) the lawyers emphasized it: "Thou shalt not *swear* falsely, but shalt perform to the Lord what thou hast *sworn*"—a man was strictly bound by an *oath* but not by a mere promise or declaration. It was explained further that an oath differed from a promise or a declaration by invoking God, directly or indirectly; and that God was named indirectly when a man swore by something specially sacred. And the definition of "specially sacred" was incredibly complicated; if a Jew said, "I swear by the gift on the Altar," he took an oath, but if he said, "I swear by the Altar," he only made a promise (§52).

Such quibbling Jesus swept away. Everything is related to God (the quotations in §29 are from Isaiah 66: 1 and Psalm 48: 2), and therefore to swear by *anything* is to swear by God. More than this, men are obliged to tell the truth in any case, oath or no oath; consequently the practice of swearing, which makes men think that a mere "yes" or "no" is not binding, is an evil thing.

Here again the words are addressed to the individual conscience; the Jews of the time were in the habit of attesting almost every statement in daily life by an oath-formula. The comparatively rare case of the administration of an oath by legal authority is probably not considered.

The saying does not relate directly to what we call "profanity," the use of sacred Names as ejaculations; but this habit is evil because it tends to make divine things meaningless.

31

In the Seventh Commandment (quoted exactly from Exodus 20: 14) the danger again was a lawyers' emphasis that would make it condemn only the flagrant act. But the impure thought, even if less serious, is just as truly wrong (compare §12).

32

"Scribes" and "Pharisees" are so frequently associated that we may forget that they were not the same thing: the scribes were a small group of very learned men who taught the Law, the Pharisees were a much larger group (around 6,000) of men, not necessarily learned, who pledged themselves to follow every letter of the Law. (Most scribes, however, were Pharisees as well.) The danger of Pharisaism lay in the fact that minute observance of the letter might obscure the spirit that lay behind the letter (§49, etc.), and an example of this error is given here.

Under the primitive conditions when Moses' Law was given, women were regarded as the property of their fathers before marriage and of their husbands afterward; and insistence on the Law's letter perpetuated this condition into New Testament times. A woman did not "marry" her husband but was "given in marriage" to him by her father. A man could divorce his wife at any time and was not required to give any reason for his action, but a woman could not divorce her husband under any conditions. In only one regard did the Law give married women some protection when divorced: by Deuteronomy 24: 1-4 the husband must renounce his authority forever and must hand her a written certificate that she was now a free woman.

This passage, however, the Pharisees interpreted as giving permission to divorce at will—according to a famous Pharisee, "if a man should find another woman fairer than his wife"—and in their argument with Jesus they used it as their "proof-text." But Jesus met them on their own ground by likewise citing a proof-text (Genesis 2: 24). It is here, He said, that God's ideal of marriage is set forth; the Deuteronomy passage was meant only as a curb on the misconduct of hardhearted men. God created men and women for lifelong marriage.

There are other sayings of Jesus on the same theme recorded in the Gospels. But their relation to the present passage and to one another is too complicated for discussion here. And so is the problem of the exceptions—if any—that Jesus might have allowed in special cases.

33-35

In §§3-32 special vices and virtues are discussed, but the present sections return to the single theme of §§1-2. Actions are determined by character; and character is determined by purpose in life.

In the last line of §35 "that darkness" is spiritual darkness, which is the worst darkness of all.

36-37

A man who has a burning purpose in life will sacrifice everything else in order to gain it; and will do so joyfully. Whether this purpose is bad or good makes no difference: in the first of these little stories the man is hardly honest, and in the second the merchant is merely businesslike. But should any purpose be more compelling than eternal life with God?

38

The "narrow" and the "wide" gates are the ways of unselfishness and of selfishness. Perhaps "few" will always prefer the former; even though Jesus was speaking primarily of the Jews of His time, in whom their teachers had implanted false ideals.

39-40

Jesus taught that in order to be "good" it is not enough to be "sinless"; the essence of goodness is activity (§§2-3), not mere abstinence from evil. "Good," therefore, in its absolute sense can be applied only to God, since He alone is perfectly active. Perhaps the inquirer really had kept the Ten Commandments. But these are negative; the real question was had he used all his powers positively? Jesus tested him by offering him a unique opportunity: "Come; I will make you one of my apostles!" (§115, etc.); but the man preferred a life of comfort.

Riches may make a man selfish, covetous, or dishonest, but their more subtle peril is a blunting of higher ambi-

tions. In any case Jesus found such small response from
the wealthy that He stated His experience in the famous
saying of §39; a saying whose severity cannot be avoided by
explaining that "camel" really means "rope" or that
"needle's eye" was a gate in Jerusalem. Yet God's power
can do what men's power cannot (§106), and at least once
Jesus met a rich man whom He could praise wholeheartedly
(§94).

41

This story—perhaps the account of an actual happening—
must have been told with a smile: the steward was a rogue,
but a most ingenious rogue; if only men would use equal
ingenuity in spiritual matters!   (Compare §37.)

In a large household the "steward" was the servant of
highest rank, who had general charge of his master's affairs;
this particular steward has proved himself dishonest or in-
competent. He knows he can never get another position
of trust, and the only alternatives seem to be manual labor
or beggary. But he thinks up a clever scheme. Men are
in debt to his master for large amounts—"a hundred measures of oil" would be about eight hundred gallons and a
"hundred measures of wheat" around one thousand bushels
—and as steward he holds their promises to pay. As he says
"Take your promise" he hands it to the debtor in question,
who grants himself a substantial rebate—and in return will
be expected to offer the steward prolonged hospitality later
on.

42

The worst sin of all is that which causes others to sin;
the worst murder of all is the murder of another person's
soul.

43

Men sometimes plead, "My nature requires certain indulgences." Such a nature must be reformed at any cost.

44

Jesus' teaching is permanently true because He never confused eternal principles with the surface problems of individual cases. In this instance the technical issues were not Jesus' affair, and the Jews had proper courts for settling such matters. But if covetousness had been avoided (§22), the brothers never would have quarreled.

45

The "tribute" was a tax laid by Rome on Jews living under direct Roman rule (that is, in southwest Palestine but not in Galilee or the rest of the country) as a token that they were Roman subjects; it must therefore be paid in Roman money. Although it amounted to only a denarion (§6) a year for each adult under sixty-five, many Jews argued that to pay it violated the Law of Moses: God's people should be subject to God alone. Jesus replied that to admit an indisputable fact can be no violation of man's duty to God; and that Rome's rule over the Jews was such a fact.

The "Herodians" were Jerusalem business men and politicians, in favor of "stable government" and so supporters of Rome's authority. They took Jesus for a political radical, who by flattery might be tempted to denounce the Romans publicly; if He had done so, His arrest and execution would have followed immediately.

46

In the first Beatitude "poor" does not mean "lacking money" but (as is indicated by the traditional phrase "poor in spirit") is used in a technical Hebrew sense: "humbled by oppression but bravely trusting in God," a meaning virtually identical with "persecuted for righteousness' sake" in the final Beatitude. Psalm 25 furnishes an excellent illustration, especially in verses 16-22; the actual word (or one indistinguishable from it in the original language) occurs in verse 9 as "meek." Compare Isaiah 61: 1 (§161).

In the second Beatitude the "mourning" that is praised is of course not for worldly but for spiritual distress. In the third "meek" is much better rendered "gentle," while "the earth" should be "the (Promised) Land." Jesus always said "Kingdom of God," but Matthew generally replaces "God" by "Heaven" in accord with a reverent Jewish custom.

When these changes are made, the marvelous structure of the Beatitudes is clearer. The promises in the second part of each all mean the same thing: to be (fully) "comforted," to "inherit the Promised Land," to be "filled" with right-eousness, to "obtain mercy," to "see God," to be "called 'Sons of God'," and to have "the Kingdom of God" are identical promises.

The second, fourth and sixth Beatitudes describe the inner character of the righteous: evil distresses them; they know they are sinners but long to become better; and their hearts are fixed on a single purpose. The third, fifth, and seventh Beatitudes describe their outward character: they are gentle, merciful and peacemakers. The first and the eighth Beatitudes "frame" the whole: in any civilization whose ideal is success at any cost such persons are bound to be despised and maltreated.

It may be interesting to know that when the Beatitudes are translated back in the language (Aramaic) used by Jesus, they appear as rhymed couplets in strict meter.

47-69

It was the failing of the Jews at Jesus' time—and of count-less human beings at every time—that so much attention might be paid to the externals of religion that its inner de-mands were forgotten. The Old Testament sets forth the loftiest ideals for men; but it also sets forth an immense number of ceremonial rules. These, past question, were really useful in helping the Jews remember that they were specially chosen by God and in helping them learn obedi-ence. Every religious group in the world, Christian or non-Christian, has found rules of some sort needful; and a purely "spiritual" (in the sense of "formless") religion probably cannot exist. Jesus Himself practiced the Old Testament ceremonies.

The difficulty is—and always will be—that so many men think superficially: it is very much easier to adopt a practice than to dwell on a spiritual truth. So one of the most mournful aspects of human history is found in the violent controversies that have raged over purely external matters; over the doing—or the *not* doing—things that in themselves are of no conceivable importance. This type of mind—known as "legalistic"—which regards specific ceremonies as of vital consequence was exhibited typically by the Pharisees; but it is exhibited likewise by narrow-minded partisans of every type of religion everywhere.

47

No external ceremony can have eternal value. Of course this does not mean that external rules are all pointless; in many instances they are necessary or, at least, helpful for a special purpose. But what God demands eternally are a pure heart, pure words, pure acts.

In the present case Jesus does not tell the Jews that they may eat pork, which the Old Testament prohibited (Leviticus 11: 7, etc.); He declares simply that observance of the Old Testament food laws will not by itself bring holiness. But when Christianity passed to the non-Jews, it was wholly in keeping with Jesus' teaching for the apostles to declare that these people were not bound by the Old Testament rules.

48

In the Authorized Version "strain *at*" a gnat was an accidental misprint, never corrected, for "strain *out*." The figure is a cup full of liquid, from which the Pharisee carefully strains out the tiny gnat but does not see the huge camel (an "unclean" animal) floating on the surface!

(Orientals love such exaggerated pictures; compare §§10, 39.)

49

The "tithe" (Leviticus 27: 30, etc.) was a tenth part of the value of agricultural produce (including livestock) raised in Palestine; this must be given to God. "Mint, anise, and cummin" were used only for seasoning, and were therefore raised in such small quantities that computing the microscopic tithe was not only a ridiculous but a difficult task; one that took so much energy as to leave none for the important virtues.

50

The scrupulous washings (Mark 7: 3-4, etc.) practiced by Pharisees before eating had nothing to do with what we call "hygiene"; what was dreaded was some kind of religious defilement for which God might punish them. Yet they forgot that to make money by sharp practices is infinitely more defiling; and it was with money so acquired that they bought the food to put into the carefully cleansed cup and platter.

51

Another saying on the same theme, more sharply and directly worded.

52

Compare §§29-30. A Pharisee believed that God would not punish him—or would not punish him much—if he deceived another person by taking an oath in a formula that did not "bind" him.

53

Since the Fourth Commandment bade men "rest," the Pharisees argued that this duty was supreme, quite apart from its effect on men; unless there was actual danger of death "work" of any kind was prohibited. Jesus replied that to God the effect of the Commandment on men was all-important, for it was given for man's sake. Therefore man was "master" of the Sabbath, could set it aside without sin to fulfill a higher duty.

In the last line the traditional "son of man" is simply a synonym for "man," as in Psalm 8: 4.

54

Since a law must be "bad" that does not permit "good," only one answer was possible to this ironic question.

55

According to the Pharisaic principles of that time a beast might be relieved on the Sabbath but a sick man must wait twenty-four hours.

56

The reference is to 1 Samuel 21: 1-6. When David and his men were in need and hungry, the only food available was the sacred show-bread (Leviticus 24: 5-9, etc.). But to God relief of hunger is more important than observing a ceremonial rule; therefore the Old Testament records David's act with approval. Consequently, Jesus' followers, when they too were hungry, could disregard the ceremonial Sabbath rule in the same way; and the same principle would apply to any other hungry men, whether followers of Jesus or not.

57

The principle underlying §§53-57, the nature of God, is here made explicit by quoting Hosea 6: 6. The Pharisees themselves regarded sacrifice as more important than the Sabbath rest, since the Law required priests to offer special sacrifices on that day (Numbers 28: 9-10). But mercy is still more important!

The traditional "One greater than the Temple" is wrong (compare the marginal reading in the Revised Version). It was not the presence of Jesus but the presence of human need that took precedence of the Sabbath.

58

The "tradition" of the scribes was made up of decisions by approved teachers, living and dead; this, the scribes claimed, was the true and inerrant interpretation of the Law. In this case the scribes had been asked, "If a man swears to do nothing for his parents, is he obliged to keep this oath?" The reply was that an oath must not be broken, no matter how much suffering it might cause. (This ruling was actually made and was still in force two centuries after Jesus' time, although after that it was changed.)

Jesus replied that this "tradition" was no interpretation of the Law but a point-blank contradiction of the Law (Exodus 20: 12; 21: 17); in such a ruling the worthlessness of the "tradition" was pitilessly revealed.

59

To the long list of decisions in the "tradition" new ones were constantly added without ever canceling any of the old ones, so that every year more and more rules were taught to a bewildered people; at the same time the teachers were cheapening the essential demands of God's righteousness (§3, etc.). Under such conditions how could anyone find his way to God?

60-61

Two sayings that teach the same moral in different figures.

62

A man brought up in a defective religion may come to realize its defects, but a man converted to it in mature life may take those very defects for virtues.

63

The bitter sarcasm of this saying is hard to convey in English. To the Oriental, "father" means both "ancestor" and "model"; "when you say 'our fathers' you say 'our models' and admit that you are like them!" Extravagant attention paid to the vices of other generations—or of other people—is fatally apt to blind us to our own vices (§10).

64

Of all hypocrisy the most loathsome form is that which demands deference and privilege in the name of religion.

Others than Pharisees sometimes see nothing inconsistent in foreclosing a mortgage on a poor woman and then attending church.

65

Publicans and harlots might be won to a sense of their sin. But the Pharisees were so convinced of their own righteousness (§89) that not even Jesus could touch their hearts. The most fatal obstacle to repentance is a sense of assured respectability. Compare §90.

66-69

Compare §59. In §67 "leaven" is explained as "hypocrisy" in Luke 12: 1 and as "teaching" in Matthew 16: 12; both are right. In §69 the "prophets" are simply the scribes and Pharisees of the preceding sections. A distorted moral standard must result in a distorted moral life.

70

It is partly true that "virtue is its own reward" and "vice is its own punishment." But both have endless further results as well, since sooner or later each soul must come face to face with God. If there is any likeness of nature (§3), the soul will be received by the Father; if there is no such likeness, the soul must suffer the consequences of its own choice.

The summons in this verse continues what nearly all Jews already believed and what the Baptist had proclaimed (§a); since the Kingdom was at hand, the Last Judgment was at hand and only repentance could deliver a guilty soul. And events were soon to show that for the Jews the warning was no "adventist" delusion. Not merely as individuals but as a nation they were called on now to make their choice. If they lived on as they were living, in the dream that because they were Abraham's children they were certain of God's protection and were entitled to despise other people, an eternal catastrophe was awaiting them. And it came. Forty years after Jesus' death their Temple was in ruins, never to be rebuilt, and Jerusalem in desolation; and from that time to this Jewish national existence has ceased from the earth.

What befell the Jews has befallen many another nation also; the same Judgment is always at hand. And it is equally at hand for individuals at every moment, in every decision of life, in every crisis of life—and in death, the unescapable end of every life.

71

The last word in this saying corresponds to an Aramaic term that can mean "soul," "life," or "self." But since in §§72-74 the stories are all taken from human events, probably the same is true here also, making "life" the best rendition: if a man dies at the moment of a worldly triumph, what good is his success to him? Compare §27.

72

If a man has no chance of winning a lawsuit, it is folly not to compromise it before it comes into court. How much greater folly it is to face God's Judgment unprepared!

The "adversary," the "officer," the "prison" and "paying the last penny" are simply parts of the story and no "spiritual" meaning is to be sought for them.

73

§§71-72 were perhaps addressed to individuals, but this section and the next are spoken to the nation. The reckless patriotism of the Jews was driving them fast into a war with Rome, whose end must be destruction. They boasted of

their skill in predicting the devastating storms (§87) and
burning heat-waves of the country; why did they not see
the approach of this infinitely worse calamity?

74

Certain Galileans were carrying their offerings into the
Temple when Pilate, the Roman governor, sent his soldiers
to kill them then and there. (Why we do not know, but
the Galileans were especially ready to rebel against Rome.)
At another time a tower in Jerusalem, near the Pool of
Siloam, collapsed and killed eighteen men in its fall. (Both
these events were evidently recent when Jesus spoke.)

The Jews were apt to regard any great misfortune as a
proof of great sinfulness (John 9: 2, etc.); but the whole
nation was standing on the brink of an unspeakable
catastrophe.

75

The real moral of this story is in the final paragraph.
What precedes is a tale of which the Jews were very fond
and one told in many ways to illustrate the difference between this life and the next; this Jesus took and retold,
merely sharpening the reasons for the fate of the two men.
"Lazarus," the name of the beggar, means "righteous";
not all beggars are good men, but he was one. The rich
man's sin was neglect of misery at his door: Lazarus not only
failed to find food but was subjected to the defiling contact
of dogs (one of the worst shames known to Orientals).

After death each received the fruits of his life. The traditional "Abraham's bosom" to which Lazarus was carried
needs explanation: the imagery is that of a banquet, at
which the guests lay on couches, leaning on the left elbow
and so spaced that a man's head came opposite his left-
hand neighbor's breast; the former was then said to be "in"
the latter's "bosom" (John 13: 23). Lazarus was given a
supreme place of honor. The rich man went to the place

of punishment which the Jews represented as inflicted by
fire, although often only as a temporary chastisement; as to
this nothing is said here.   But be that as it may, heartless
selfishness brings terrible consequences that cannot be escaped.

To this tale, already familiar to His hearers, Jesus adds a
new ending. In the Bible the Jews were taught the truth; if
they did not pay attention to it, nothing could help them,
not even a miracle: moral change must come from within.

76

The moral of §75 in explicit language.

77

The purest light of all is given in Jesus' teaching; to acknowledge this with our lips but not in our lives is utter
hypocrisy.

78-81

Four sayings on different aspects of the same theme.   A
man who has never had a chance is excusable but not a man
to whom opportunity is given; and the greater the opportunity, the greater the responsibility. Yet great opportunity
is given only after the soul has proved itself in lesser matters; success or failure in these determines future possi-
bilities.

82

The theme of §§80-81 is developed in a lengthy story. A
man engaged in large affairs tests his assistants to see if they
are fit for increased responsibilities. Two of them meet
the test and are duly promoted; the third, however, fails
and tries to cover up his failure by abusing his master. But
he does not believe his own words: if he had really thought
his master was so dangerous a man, he would have been
frightened into action of some sort—at least into the most
obvious way of increasing the sum put in his charge.

On "talent" compare §21; it is from the present story that the word has in English come to mean any natural gift given to a man. Banks in the ancient world paid a high rate of interest (8 per cent or more).

Since to Jesus the essence of goodness is activity, failure to use one's abilities is always inexcusable (§40). Everyone has an opportunity of some sort; at least the talent may always be "put in the bank," the ordinary routine of life may be lived more generously and more usefully. But to say "I have done no harm" is never enough.

83

Relapse after moral reformation makes an almost hopeless condition.

The story is told in terms that the common people of Palestine would understand: insane persons may sometimes have lucid intervals that are followed by violent mania. In folklore demons are thought to be afraid of water (compare the tales of Tam O'Shanter and Ichabod Crane) and therefore wander only in "waterless places."

84-86

By Jesus' hearers these warnings were understood of the Last Judgment, but they are just as true of every other Judgment, whether on individuals or on nations: no one can know at what moment he may be confronted by a crisis that may change his entire future. Moral watchfulness, therefore, must never be relaxed for a moment.

§86 pictures a custom of the time. When a bridegroom brought home his bride (the words "and the bride" belong in the passage), etiquette required him to invite in and entertain all the girls of the village who met him with lighted lamps. Despite the gravity of the warning Jesus tells the story almost playfully (compare §41), making it turn about the passion girls everywhere have for anything connected with weddings.

87

Religion is worthless unless it is built on a solid foundation of righteousness.

In Palestine rain normally falls only twice a year, in December (the "former rains") and in March (the "latter rains"), but in those months the country is deluged and the watercourses flooded. A builder skimping foundation-work might put up a house that looked strong in the dry season, but it would go to pieces as soon as the rains undermined it. Jesus speaks as an experienced carpenter.

II

THE FATHER

88-89

These two sections should be studied together. The essential quality in childlikeness is the absence of the bargaining instinct: a child does not argue, "Because I have been a good boy I have earned my food and clothing from my father." These things are the gifts of the father's affection; attempts to force this affection—or to win pardon for a fault—by self-conscious and priggish good behavior are ruinous to childhood. When a little boy observes "I am much better than my brothers and sisters," he shows that something is very wrong with him.

It was just this attitude that the Pharisee took in his prayer to God. All he says, perhaps, is truthful enough. He might really have kept the negative Commandments of the Law (compare §40). He can likewise boast that in two regards he has gone beyond the Law's demands: in addition to the one yearly fast enjoined (Leviticus 16: 29, etc.) he has kept two voluntary fasts every week (§99), and he has paid tithes not only on agricultural produce (§49) but on his entire income. He is perfectly self-satisfied—but only because his conception of God is a being like himself; of God's immeasurable majesty and holiness he has not the slightest idea. Only God is "good"! (§40.)

90

Compare §65. The Pharisees were loud in protestations of their desire to please God but ignored His righteousness; the publicans and harlots had turned away from God but turned back to Him in repentance.

91

God's rewards to men are not measured by our merits but by His generosity; in heaven the formula "so-much for so-much" is no longer true.

On "denarion" compare §6; this sum was the normal day's wage for unskilled labor. At the grape harvest many extra hands were needed. The order of the payment was a mere whim of the householder, but if the laborers who had been hired first had been paid first, they would not have seen the extra pay given to the late-comers. With the former's envy of the householder's generosity compare the elder brother's attitude in §98.

The story nowadays is sometimes read as if it meant that all men on earth should receive a living wage. Of course in a Christian society no one should be allowed to suffer want, but Jesus told the story for a different reason.

92

Not only could a despised publican (§4) be assured of God's pardon, but Jesus could use such a one in the high service of personal discipleship (§114).

93

Since a physician's place is among the sick, Jesus' place was among the sinners who needed His help. Whether or not any really "well" persons exist is not discussed.

94

We are not told how Jesus recognized Zacchaeus; perhaps by asking who this man was who seemed so anxious to see Him. Since no religious teacher of the day would enter Zacchaeus's house, he must have rebelled against all religion until Jesus treated him so generously.

In §40 the rich man was capable of heroism, and Jesus called on him to show it; the more commonplace Zacchaeus was not disturbed in his occupation.

95

Another poor soul won by Jesus' gentleness.

At a formal Jewish meal the guests reclined on couches (§75) with their feet extended toward the space between these couches and the wall. "Pious" Jews left the housedoor open and allowed beggars to enter and stand in this space, in the hope that someone might pass them food. The poor woman, therefore, came in unhindered; Jesus had assured her that she was God's child and she showed her gratitude as best she could. Was it not natural that so great a sinner should be grateful for forgiveness?

The remainder of the story in Luke (7: 44-50) is told in terms that need elaborate explanation for modern readers.

96-97

These stories brought something new to the Judaism of the time. The Jews knew from the Old Testament that God would willingly forgive anyone who repented; but they always pictured God as waiting for the sinner to come to Him. It was Jesus who revealed that God searches for the sinner before he even thinks of returning.

98

This story—no doubt the most familiar of all that Jesus told—is often partially misunderstood by taking the father to represent God directly. But this father is a very human father: not very wise, for he lets his boy go out into the world with his pockets full of money and no one to guide him. And not very considerate, for he has taken his hard-working and obedient elder son too much for granted. The precise point is that if such a father could be so awakened to demonstrative love, *how much more* will the Heavenly Father go to meet a returning prodigal?

Jewish fathers could not dispose of their property by will: at their death it must be divided among all the sons evenly, except that the oldest received a double share (Deuteronomy 21: 17); consequently, the elder of two sons would take two thirds and the younger one third. Here the younger was given his share in advance, but the story shows that after the "division" the father kept control of the rest and the older son got nothing.

The boy's experiences were only what might have been expected; and he sank to herding pigs (to the Jews a filthy occupation). The traditional "husks" that the swine ate were the pods of the carob bean; a good fodder but edible by human beings only when ravenously hungry. These pods were fed from a carefully guarded store to the pigs, who had a high market value; the food given to the boy—who had no market value—was pitiful in contrast. When he came to his senses, he went home, with a thoroughly rehearsed speech on his lips. This his father's joy interrupted; a banquet was prepared and made as joyous as possible (the "dancing" was by professional entertainers, not by the household).

But in the enthusiasm the older son was completely forgotten, something that must have increased his astonished anger when he learned what was happening; what he said to his father was uncharitable but natural enough under the circumstances. The father's reply is a real apology, and he makes amends: the faithful elder son is precious to him indeed. None the less his happiness over this other boy is more than justified.

99

Our motive in a religious act may be to serve God or to win praise from men. But it cannot be both.

The beautiful structure of this saying consists in a general truth developed in three parallel applications. The word translated "religious acts" ("alms" in the Authorized Version is wrong) is used by Jews to describe almsgiving, prayer and fasting taken together. The next to the last lines in the second and third applications have been re-translated from the Aramaic; "in secret" describes the

prayer or fasting, not the Father. The Authorized Version's
addition of "openly" at the end of each application is
wrong; the reward given is "secret"—between the soul and
God.

Fasting was regarded by the Jews as a voluntary act of
self-discipline with real religious value (§89). This Jesus
does not deny; nevertheless, He and His disciples did not
practice it (§139).

100

In Luke's Gospel (11: 2-4) the Lord's Prayer has a shorter
form than in Matthew (6: 9-13). The latter is clearer and
has passed into Christian use, but Luke's wording contains
everything essential. In Aramaic the opening word was
"Abba" (Mark 14: 36, Romans 8: 15, Galatians 4: 6), which
could mean either "Father" or "Our Father," but there is
of course no real difference. Nor does it matter whether
"Who art in heaven" is taken for granted or said explicitly.

Since Jewish prayers almost always open with thanksgiving, the second clause is best understood in this sense:
"We thank Thee that Thou hast made Thyself known to
us;" God's "Name" is His Nature as revealed to men. But
since every act of God is a revelation the clause can be
translated equally well: "We thank Thee for all Thou hast
done for us."

God's Kingdom "comes" (§a) when His purpose for man
is perfectly fulfilled; as Matthew puts it, when His will is
"done on earth as it is in heaven."

On taking each day by itself compare §109; on the relation between forgiveness and forgivingness §§14-21. And
the final petition is that we may not only be "delivered
from evil" but from every approach to evil.

101-102

It is only necessary to remember that God alone knows
what gifts are really "good" for us; often we pray for stones
but God gives us bread.

103

Even though God knows our needs, a child cannot help speaking to its Father. But the naturalness of the relation will be spoiled if any stress is laid on the form of words used; even the Lord's Prayer is no "efficacious" formula.

104-105

The other aspect of the truth of §103; every father wants his children to tell him freely what is in their hearts, even though he knows what it is. If on earth persistence will wring favors from reluctant givers, how much more is God ready to hear us!

106-108

Often so much time is spent on explaining the obvious limitations of these sayings (compare especially §209) that their positive truth may be obscured: how great this truth is only they who live the prayer-life know.

109

Again Jesus' tone is almost playful (§86) but again the truth is profound; full trust in the power of God will leave the future in His hands.

110

Food alone will not preserve life (§27) nor will clothing alone give health to the body; more is needed, and this "more" is God's will—the one thing utterly essential, but the one thing we constantly forget. The man who earnestly tries to do God's will—who "seeks the Kingdom"—may be sure that God will give him everything needed for the work he has to do; and that God's help will continue until that work is finished.

In the older English of the Authorized Version "take no thought" means exactly the same as the modern "be not anxious;" Jesus does not mean "do not think about it at all," but "do not worry about it." But the Authorized Version's "add one cubit to his stature" was a blunder. "Stature" should be "course of life," the path we tread all our days; and to prolong such a path by a mere "cubit" (about 18 inches) would be to prolong life by less than a second of time. (Indeed, worry shortens life instead of lengthening it.)

The "lilies" of Palestine are purple and scarlet, like the robes of Eastern kings. Dried grass was literally "cast into the oven," to heat it before baking.

111

A human little story, whose correct wording is given in the margin of the Revised Version. Martha, like many good women the world over, felt that she must honor a distinguished visitor by an enormous meal; forgetting that this made her treat the food as more important than Jesus' teaching. Not that the food was to be neglected entirely; this, too, would have been a fault. But a few simple dishes—or even only one—would have been quite enough.

112

The Sadducees were a small group of wealthy and extremely aristocratic Jews. Like most aristocrats they were intensely conservative, refusing to accept the belief in a future life which other Jews adopted late in the Old Testament period. So they came to Jesus with a "catch-question," based on Deuteronomy 25: 5-10: if a married Jew died childless, his brother took the widow; and any children born of this union were considered the offspring of the dead man.

Jesus might have met them on their own level by replying that in all the marriages the woman was still counted as the legal wife of her first husband; but His reply brushed quibbling aside and went to the heart of the matter. When the Sadducees talked about "marriage in the world to come," they showed their petty conception of God's power: the eternal life He will give His children is of a wholly different kind. And Exodus 3: 6 shows that this life is a certainty; to allow the saints who had served Him to pass into nothingness would be utterly unworthy of God, whose very nature, therefore, gives men eternal hope.

113

No effective living is possible without discipline (a "yoke") of some sort; but the discipline demanded by the teachers of the day had become unendurable (§59, etc.). To be sure, the discipline that Jesus exacts (§§1-46) may try the beginner sorely; but it will prove itself the easiest of all.

III

THE MISSION

114-117

Every Jewish teacher had a group of students who lived with him, attended to his needs and accompanied him wherever he went; these were known as his "disciples" ("learners"). Or, since they always walked behind him, they were also said to "come after him" or "follow him." Jesus' summons, "Follow me," was therefore a call to discipleship in a similar sense; whoever obeyed the summons must give up his former life, in order to serve Jesus and to learn from Him. But since, unlike the other teachers, Jesus' mission was to preach, His disciples were trained to preach also. And while learning the complicated tradition of the other teachers involved a discipleship of many years, the simpler teaching of Jesus could be mastered in a short time.

Among these disciples a special group of twelve (§117) received a special call and training. But there were others also—how many is not recorded—and the number might be added to at any time (§40).

We—and perhaps in some degree the Gospels likewise—also use "disciple" more widely, to describe anyone who accepted Jesus' teaching and tried to follow it; like Mary in §111 or Zacchaeus in §94. But neither Mary nor Zacchaeus was a "disciple" in the more technical sense: preaching by a woman was unthinkable to Jews, and Jesus did not give Zacchaeus the special call. This double use of the word sometimes creates confusion: often Jesus' sayings are made unduly harsh—as when the words in §123 are taken to be addressed to everyone—or become incomprehensible—as when the words in §§125-126 are applied in the same way. Such confusion may be avoided if "disciple" in the stricter sense is explained as "missionary" in the first three Gospels (the use in the fourth Gospel is different); and under modern conditions be understood to mean those undertaking a life of special dedication.

It is helpful to know that all the disciples, including the Twelve, were probably younger than Jesus; Peter, for instance, was active as a missionary for more than a generation after Jesus' death. (Artists in depicting the Twelve in Jesus' lifetime forget this.)

118

Self-denial—refusal to take the way easiest for self—is necessary for all who try to live rightly (§43, etc.). But it was doubly necessary for the missionaries. "Be my disciple" and "follow me" mean exactly the same thing.

119

Hospitality, especially when extended to a teacher, was a virtue highly esteemed by the Jews. So the missionaries could expect to have their wants supplied (§§147-149), and carrying money would show lack of faith in God (§110). But when conditions changed, Jesus gave the missionaries different instructions (§208).

120-122

Three concrete cases: one of too much enthusiasm, the others of too much hesitation. Unless a man was fully prepared to give himself wholly to the work he would be a failure; Jesus' time was very short and the crisis the greatest in the world's history.

To the first listener the traditional "son of man" could have meant only "man" (§53); the wild animals had better protection than Jesus had. In the other cases mere family courtesies were put above the pressing needs of the souls in Galilee. At a father's funeral a son was obliged to touch the dead body and was thereby made "unclean" for seven days (Numbers 19), but Jesus' work could not wait a week or more; there were plenty of persons with no sense of a spiritual call who would conduct the burial. And Jesus had had personal experience of the well-meant interference of families (§177).

123

Compare §§40, 94.

124

Jews valued marriage so highly that an unmarried man was felt to be lacking in his religious duty. But God had called Jesus to a still higher duty that made marriage impossible; and this same call might well come to some of the missionaries also. Even then, however, they would only make a sacrifice that other men have had to make unwillingly.

125-126

The warning in these stories is addressed solely to would-be missionaries (§120) and not to Jesus' other disciples. There can be no counting the cost in following the way of righteousness; for this cost must be borne, whether a man will or no (§43, etc.). But before undertaking the still greater cost of missionary work, each man must measure his abilities very carefully; since failure there will be disastrous for others as well as for himself.

127

The missionaries must not expect better treatment than Jesus Himself received, nor better success in their work. That all men can be converted by the right appeal is grossly untrue; Jesus Himself could not convert everyone. When obstinate evil is confronted with good it is aroused to hatred and violence; Jesus' enemies actually said that He was inspired by the devil (§166). The missionaries, therefore, must not be surprised or discouraged at the bitterly unjust treatment they may receive. Compare §140.

This saying need not be confined to the missionaries, for

everyone who tries to live rightly may meet with similar opposition.

"Beelzebub," originally the name of a heathen god (2 Kings 1), was used by the Jews as a contemptuous title for Satan.

128-129

The tension created by Jesus' preaching made itself felt even within families, setting the older generation against the younger. Presumably the younger people would be more affected by Jesus' preaching and would be regarded by their elders as radicals, but this situation might be reversed in some cases. The quotation is from Micah 7: 6.

A married Jewish girl was expected to give her husband's mother perfect respect and obedience.

130

In Jesus' lifetime only the missionaries were likely to suffer actual arrest and condemnation by the authorities, but in the next generation any disciple ran the same danger.

Outside of Jerusalem Jewish courts met in the synagogue buildings, and sentences of scourging (Deuteronomy 25: 1-3, etc.) were carried out then and there. Palestine was ruled by Roman "governors" and Herodian "kings"; the missionaries should rejoice at the opportunity given them to speak to persons otherwise inaccessible.

131

Every disciple of Jesus, whether carrying on a special work or living a quiet life, is always being watched by others; and any failure on his part will be noted instantly.

132-133

Cowardly suppression of any part of Jesus' message is inexcusable. And such suppression is always useless; the truth is bound to come to light. But compare §§150-151.

134-135

Salt and light have no value in themselves; the purpose of salt is to season other things and the purpose of light to illumine other objects. So any disciple of Jesus, whether a missionary or not, who does not affect those around him is no disciple at all: Jesus recognizes goodness only when it is active.

The "lamp" of the period was a flat, oval vessel of metal or clay, burning olive oil by means of a wick at one end; the "stand" might be a small table or a wall-bracket. "Candles" (as in the Authorized Version) were unknown. A large measure ("bushel") for grain or flour was found in every house.

136-138

To preach or live Jesus' message might bring a man into grave danger; but not to preach or live it was infinitely more dangerous. In §138 "Son of Man" was the Jewish title for the heavenly Messiah who would hold the Last Judgment (§213, etc.; compare §§a-b).

139

The insistence of §§114-138 on the utter seriousness of the missionary task and the deep responsibilities of the missionaries is so intense as to be almost terrifying. But the joyful sense of the privilege was deeper yet; the sense of an opportunity such as the world had never known; the realization of being not only a child of God but chosen by Jesus to be a coworker with God. For such men to fast would have been as inconsistent as gloom at a marriage feast; for them to take up the mournful custom again would have been as senseless as spoiling an old garment by a new patch or of pouring new wine in old wineskins. Compare §§142, 165.

On fasting among the Jews compare §§89, 99. When a bridegroom left his wedding banquet it was a signal that the feast was over. "New" (wool) cloth shrinks; and if sewed to old cloth will tear itself away when the shrinkage occurs. In the ancient world wine, when not stored in jars, was kept in the skins of small animals; and only flexible new skins could stand the strain of the fermenting new wine.

These sayings probably apply primarily to the missionaries; but they would be true also of anyone who has learned from Jesus that he can trust securely in the Father's Love and care (§110, etc.).

140

Opposition from evil men is not only inevitable (§127) but may be a proof that the man they oppose is truly Jesus' messenger and therefore God's servant. Such opposition should then be a source of joy.

141

Since God's protection is always around those who serve Him (§110), how much more will He not protect those who devote their whole lives to His special work?

142

The service of Jesus is not a painful duty to be endured for the sake of happiness hereafter; the service itself brings with it happiness here and now: the missionaries, despite all their hardships, found a delight in their work far greater than any riches could give them. Compare §§36-37, 139.

143

Men about to be tried for an offense liable to the death penalty are often in a state of panic before the trial; they exhaust themselves trying to think of ways of defending themselves. But Jesus told His missionaries not to think about that at all; they could trust in God to inspire them when the time came. On the Spirit as God's gift of power compare §b.

144

The supreme promise: they who dedicate their lives to Jesus' work shall have a unique share in Jesus' glory. The reward is pictured in vivid Old Testament imagery; Jesus is the King and the missionaries His royal princes, who eat at His table (2 Samuel 9: 7, etc.) and rule the people in His name ("judge" is used as in Judges 3: 10, etc.).

145

Even when traveling from one place to another the missionaries must keep their minds wholly concentrated on their work. Compare 2 Kings 4: 29.

146

Since God had given His promises to the Jews, Jesus' first appeal must be to them; the opportunity of other nations (§§184-185) could come later.

147-149

In work for God it is the earnest effort, not the immediate success, that counts. But the effort must be earnest; devoted only to winning souls and not to gaining greater comfort for one's self. On the other hand, no missionary should be ashamed of being poor, for what he gives men is of far greater worth than what they give him.

150

Preaching Jesus' message fearlessly and without reserve (§§132-133) does not mean blind recklessness in delivering it; its purpose is to win men, not to repel and enrage them. Jesus' enemies were on the watch for any excuse to attack the missionaries.

Serpents were regarded as the craftiest of all animals (Genesis 3: 1).

151

Some men are so degraded that preaching to them is useless or worse than useless: they will either treat God's message with utter indifference or will be roused by it to blasphemy and outrage. (For instance, Jesus did not try to appeal to the "better nature" of the Temple traders [§200].)

The first and last lines of the saying describe the vicious "dogs," the second and third the brutish "swine."

152

Jesus—perhaps half humorously—calls His missionaries "scribes," for they too were now teachers. From Him they have learned many "old" things—the real meaning of the familiar Old Testament—and many "new" things also (§17, etc.); to use in accord with the special needs of their hearers.

153

It is not the number but the quality of converts that is important. Compare §155.

154

Since the missionaries were to preach only what Jesus had taught them, their message was His as well.

155

This story can be read in two ways. It can be taken as a warning to the hearers to make sure that their hearts are not hard, shallow or thorny ground; and it is so taken in the familiar explanation that follows it in the Gospels. But it can also be taken as an encouragement to the missionaries: many men will not profit by the message, but they who do will more than make up for the others. Compare §153.

156

In the explanation that follows this story in Matthew it is applied to the Last Judgment. But it can be applied equally well to Jesus' and the missionaries' selection of disciples from among those attracted by the preaching.

IV

THE REJECTION

157

It was preaching, not healing, that was Jesus' true mission; His work was hampered by men frantically anxious about their bodies but not about their souls.

158

An experience common the world over. Persons who have associated familiarly with a man in his younger days are hurt in their pride to admit that he could have progressed while they have not.

159

A difficult saying, capable of several interpretations. But the translation given is the most probable: instead of looking for God's Kingdom as righteousness, men are trying to bring it by stirring up the nation to declare war against Rome (compare §c). It is true that the fulfillment of God's promises began with a spiritual revival preached by the Baptist. But this revival is being hopelessly perverted.

160

A man already completely self-satisfied will refuse to listen to anything new.

161

The Baptist was no "reed shaken by the wind," never able to make up his mind. Nor did he put any value on worldly display; men who do that are not found in the wilderness. He was truly a prophet, the very greatest of all the prophets. And yet he would never understand Jesus. He belonged to the old order, not the new (§191), able to think of the Messiah only as he himself had proclaimed him (§a).

Jesus' answer is a combination and expansion of Isaiah 35: 5 and 61: 1, verses that the Jews recognized as predictions of the Messiah. He said, in effect, "Can you not see that prophecy is being fulfilled?" While in this reply "blind," "lame," etc., undoubtedly have their literal sense, they have also a higher sense that is far more important: to heal a blind man is a miracle, but to give vision to the spiritually blind is an incomparably greater miracle. Compare §187.

162

In Luke's Gospel the "sign of Jonah" is the prophet's preaching (§170); when he told the Ninevites of their sin, they acknowledged it and repented. Just so Jesus' preaching was sign enough for the Jews of the day, the only sign that could possibly do them permanent good; for moral change must come from within (§75).

When in Matthew's Gospel the sign is explained as Jesus' resurrection there is little real difference, for it is only to a man moved by the preaching that the Resurrection will have meaning.

163

In many battles it is possible to be neutral, but not in the battle between good and evil.

164

A "word" spoken against Jesus is forgivable when it is spoken because of misunderstanding or ignorance (compare the Baptist's inability in §161). But no word is forgivable that men know in their consciences to be untrue but speak only to justify blind hatred; this is "blasphemy" against God's Spirit working in their hearts.

This blasphemy is illustrated in §§165-166: the teachers were so infuriated by Jesus' criticisms that they lost all sense of moral decency.

Simple souls sometimes worry themselves about this sin; but the very fact that they are worried is absolute proof that they have not committed it; where this blasphemy exists conscience is dead.

165

The teachers were so blinded by anger that they could not see that their denunciations of the Baptist and of Jesus contradicted each other.

Compare §139. Wine in Palestine was so expensive that drunkenness was a vice possible only to the very rich; the common people drank it so diluted (four or five times as much water as wine) as to be harmless. Even this was usually restricted to special occasions; but it would be used more freely by the "publicans and sinners" among whom Jesus worked and whose pleasures He shared (§93).

Conditions in the modern world, of course, are entirely different, and wholly new factors have entered into the temperance problem.

166

In this case the slander is self-contradictory. To say that Satan has taken to doing good amounts to saying that there is a revolution in his kingdom.

And the slander was absurd for another reason also. Among the Jews there were healers ("your sons") who—we may be quite certain—were occasionally successful in working cures. These men were experts: if the teachers had troubled to ask them, they would have ridiculed the possibility of working such cures "by Beelzebub." But the teachers did not want advice: all they cared for was to abuse Jesus. And so they, claiming to be God's only spokesmen, were totally blind to what God was doing in their very midst (§187).

167

There was still a chance that the people might repent;

and while the least chance remained Jesus' efforts must continue.

168-169

Compare §7.

170

For the Queen of the South ("Sheba") see 1 Kings 10: 1-10; for Jonah's preaching to Nineveh see Jonah 3-4. The traditional English versions are wrong in reading "a greater than Solomon" and "a greater than Jonah": it was Jesus' *message* that was greater than the wisdom of Solomon or the preaching of Jonah (compare the margin of the Revised Version).

Salvation was not limited to the Jews (§§168, 184-185).

171

If a single house rejects the missionaries (§147), they can go to another house; but if every house in a whole city rejects them—and Jesus with them—there is nothing more that they can do. Yet the city must be warned that God is not mocked.

To Jews the warning gesture amounted to saying, "God will treat you as a heathen city." Sodom's fate is told in Genesis 19.

172-173

Capernaum, Bethsaida, and Chorazin lay close together and it was in this district that Jesus' work centered. Such an opportunity might well have exalted these cities to heaven—but they refused it.

Tyre is often mentioned in the Old Testament as Israel's enemy (Psalm 83: 7, etc.). Sidon appears less frequently (Joshua 13: 6, etc.), but the two cities were closely associated and were regarded by the Jews as only less evil than Sodom (§171).

174

The story describes a perfectly possible occurrence: a man
finding himself left with no guests calls in the beggars to eat
his food.   Just so the ostentatiously "religious" leaders of
the Jews refused to listen to Jesus, and He turned to those
who would hear Him (§§65, 190, etc.).

Sending a servant to notify guests was an ordinary cour-
tesy of the times.

175

The application of this story—which needs no explanation—was made unmistakable by the allusions to Isaiah
5: 1-2. The contrast between the "husbandmen" and the
"others" is best understood as in §174.

In the story as it appears in the Gospels a fourth attempt
to persuade the husbandmen is added: the owner sends
his beloved son.   Jesus could have used this unmistakable
reference to Himself in telling the story to His disciples, but
hardly in a public address to His enemies, especially after
refusing to let them know by what authority He taught
(§201).

V

CONVERSION

176-177

Compare §154.

178

God's reward is not won by personal gifts but by the right use of such opportunities as may come to a man (§91). The inspired prophet and the humble individual who helps him a little in his work have both done their duty—and only their duty (§11); in God's sight, then, they are equal.

179

This saying must not be confused with that in §88, for the moral is wholly different. Here the meaning is that no missionary should boast of the number of converts he has made; to care for the soul of a single little child is as supreme an achievement in the eyes of God.

180

The reverse of §179. But "little ones" need not be limited to children, for many humble and simple grown persons are "little ones" also.

181

In §163 the point is: In the battle between good and evil there can be no inner neutrality. Here: The outward progress of Jesus' work may be helped by even very imperfect believers.

182

A missionary must have authority over his converts in order to help them—but only in order to help them. And the same is true of Christian authority of any sort.

183

This story recalls that in §82 but is told so as to apply directly to the missionaries: they are put in charge not of money but of souls. Abuse of their position, therefore, is indescribably serious.

In very large households untrustworthy slaves were kept by themselves under iron discipline.

184

To Jesus one religion was not as good as another: the Jews had been granted God's special revelation and their opportunity must come first (§146). But this woman deserves His sympathy, and He speaks to her in her own terms (the Jews, unlike the non-Jews, did not keep house dogs [§75]). Many women would have replied indignantly "We are as good as you are," but this woman does not; she knows the Jews have something her people lack, and she begs this Jew to help her. Compare §88.

185

A similar example of humility and faith.

A "centurion" ("commander of a hundred men") was a lower officer in the Roman army, corresponding roughly to the modern "first sergeant." But during Jesus' ministry no Roman troops were stationed in Galilee, so that this centurion was in Herod's (§197) service. He probably was a Roman veteran, who had been honorably discharged and then had taken a position as an officer of Herod's constabulary; so that he can be described as "chief of the Capernaum police." As such his duty made him keep a close watch on this new teacher, who impressed him deeply. Here was a man who was not blinded by prejudice!

Jesus' first reply is best read as an astonished question.

186

The deep meaning of this saying is explained in the following sections.

187

The Jews distinguished very sharply between bodily and mental diseases; and Jesus did the same. Caring for men's bodies was not His primary task (§157), for men can worship God despite physical ills. But men with sick minds are cut off from God, so that Jesus felt He owed them an imperative duty. He had extraordinary success with them, success so great that in comparison with the cures wrought by others (§166) His were "by the finger of God."

That is, through Jesus a unique divine power was now at work in the world; a power that was driving evil out of the hearts and minds of men; a supreme active goodness wholly new to mankind. What was this power? It was the first visible sign of the long-awaited Kingdom of God, at last touching the earth in the person of Jesus.

That forces from the Kingdom should herald its coming was expected by the Jews; they looked for convulsions of nature, earthquakes, tidal waves, famines, stars falling from heaven. Jesus showed them something still more wonderful —the moral transformation of human beings. Compare §161.

In the ancient world insanity was popularly explained as due to evil beings who took control of the mind of the sufferer. In the modern world very many—although not all —cases of insanity are scientifically explained as due to evil ideas which take control of the mind of the sufferer: selfishness, passion, pride, terrors. The cure consists in driving out these ideas and replacing them with wholesome truth; to drive them out without replacing them does more harm than good (§83). The overpowering personality of Jesus was able to do almost in a moment what modern specialists can do only slowly and laboriously; and today His teaching is continually a barrier against the entry of such "demons" and of priceless aid in "casting them out." Nor are "insane" persons the only ones "possessed" by such "demons"—or by others even more deadly!

188

The "strong man" is Satan; his "goods" are the souls of men; the "stronger" is Jesus.

189

What Jesus had done, now His missionaries could do: through them also the power of the Kingdom was manifested. They too, then, were citizens of that Kingdom, with their names enrolled in heaven; and in them as well as in Jesus the Kingdom was already present.

As in §144 the imagery is intensely pictorial. "I was watching" describes the time of their success; Jesus was following them in His heart. The Jews believed that Satan had gained power over this world (John 14: 30), and that he ruled over his realm from a throne in the sky (Revelation 12: 7-9). Now the missionaries had broken his power, and he was thrust from his seat with the suddenness of lightning. "Serpents" and "scorpions" are symbolic terms for his demons.

A few distressed souls had been restored to health; something apparently of little importance. But this was actually the most crucial moment in the history of the world: Jesus was no longer alone in His use of the Kingdom's power; the missionaries had it also and could communicate it to others, and they to still others indefinitely. So, no matter what might happen to Jesus, His work would go on forever.

190

The connection with §189 is immediate: the missionaries' triumph calls forth Jesus' thanksgiving. A strange thing indeed had come to pass. The "wise" and the "prudent" —the great religious leaders of the day—had turned against Jesus, and only "babes"—fishermen, farmers, publicans— had accepted Him. And yet God's purpose was perfectly fulfilled!

This, then, was God's plan, to be thankfully accepted.

And now the future was plain. All expectation about the nature of the Messiah ("Son"; compare §b) was wrong; only God knew. But now Jesus knew—and so did they whom Jesus had taught.

The traditional text of this passage is slightly longer, but the earliest evidence supports the form given; in any case the meaning is the same.

191

The Baptist was God's greatest prophet (§162), but he was not "in" the Kingdom. His teaching was inspired by God; but he never had the personal gift of spiritual power that changes other men by contact. They who are "in" the Kingdom are more than "saved" souls; they have become "saving" souls.

Jesus speaks only of His missionaries as already members of the present Kingdom. But the strength that they gained from Him could be gained by the other disciples also; it is a quality that should mark everyone who follows Him.

192

Just as the wheat grows, so will the Kingdom grow—and in both the reason for the growth is beyond man's understanding.

The "man" in this story is not Jesus but anyone who plants.

193-194

The beginning of the Kingdom seemed of no account (§189). But the beginning is no measure of the end; from a tiny mustard seed will grow a plant ten to twelve feet high; a tiny pinch of leaven will spread through "three measures" (more than a bushel) of meal.

In §194 it is tempting to think of the "meal" as the world, which Christianity will gradually penetrate and transform. But this was not the immediate purpose of the story.

195

All human expectations of the Messiah were wrong; God's purpose was very different (§190). In the Temptation (§c) He revealed that the Promised One was to be no worker of stupendous miracles to overawe men (compare §75, etc.), and no national leader to appeal to their patriotism. His work must begin and continue with an unswerving proclamation of righteousness. Nor would this preaching bring support from the nation as a whole or even from the nation's religious leaders; for help Jesus had to look to "little ones" and "babes" (§190, etc.). And indifference had grown into hostility (§150, etc.), until all Galilee was becoming dangerous (§197); to gain any peace at all Jesus had to leave Palestine proper and go into heathen country. (The capital of northeast Palestine shows by its name "Caesar's City" that the ruler Philip [Luke 3: 1] was not a good Jew.) The Promised One was forced out of the Promised Land!

But the hardest lesson was still to come. It was so terrible that Jesus tested the faith of His missionaries before He taught it to them: now that His fortunes had sunk so low, what did they think of Him? They met the test and He told them the bitter truth: His ministry must end in death. For a moment the strain on them was too great, and Peter protested—to be silenced by the sharpest rebuke that Jesus could utter. God's will was clear. Since this was the only way, it was the way by which God would accomplish His purpose.

For Matthew's longer version of this section reference must be made to the special commentaries.

196

"Fire" is used like "sword" in §128; Jesus' teaching was arousing a conflict among men. This conflict would bring His own death, but His duty was clear.

In the third line the traditional "I have a baptism to be

baptized with" does not give the sense in English; the imagery is that of Psalm 69: 2.

197

It was really Herod who sent this message, and Jesus' contemptuous "that fox" ("sly animal") shows that He saw through the trick. But Herod need not be anxious: Jesus was leaving Galilee—but because of His work, not because of Herod.

198

Although James and John were willing to face death for Jesus, they had not yet mastered His teaching: rank in the Kingdom is not given by favoritism but must be won through faithful service.

199-202

In Galilee and in Philip's territory (§195) Jesus was safe from the Jerusalem authorities, but they had determined to put Him to death if He ever came to the city. His reply was to enter Jerusalem in the most conspicuous way possible (§199), to make an onslaught on the Temple market (§200), and to treat the authorities' claim to divine guidance with public contempt (§§201-202). That is, He met their determination by challenging them to do their worst.

199

The correspondence with Zechariah 9: 9 is obvious. God's promise was fulfilled, even though Jerusalem rejected it.

200

The Temple market was established by the authorities for their own profit. Its pretense was that it supplied sacrificial animals that fulfilled the ritual requirements, but the prices charged were exorbitant and animals purchased elsewhere were refused. Moreover, in the Temple the authorities had no rent to pay; and they did not care that the noise of the animals and the haggling of the traders were destructive of devotion. This shameless business was so hated by the Jews that Jesus would have had the instant support of the crowd, and any attempt of the authorities to interfere would have caused a riot.

201

The "rulers" were the officials of the Great Sanhedrin (§12), which claimed to be the infallible interpreter of God's Law. But Jesus' reply to their demand is a test of that claim: they must prove it by settling once and for all whether the Baptist was inspired. And their "We do not know" shows how worthless their claim is; if they cannot answer that vital question, they are unfit to speak in God's name on any subject. Religious authority that fails in a crisis is no authority at all.

202

The teachers held that the Messiah would be a "son of David," like David a military leader who would defeat Israel's enemies. But they left no place for the inspired declaration of Psalm 110: 1, which depicts a Messiah of incomparably higher nature.

No other conception of the Messiah would have been possible to Jesus now that He was face to face with death. God's call could not fail; as His work could not be completed in this life, He would complete it in the world to come, from heaven.

That David wrote Psalm 110 was taken for granted in the first century. Nothing, however, depends on David's authorship, and the argument would be just as strong if Jesus had said "the Psalmist" instead of David himself; the words of this Psalm cannot describe an earthly king.

203

The accounts say that this ointment was "pure spikenard," a perfume that was very expensive; the cost of the woman's "measure" is given as "300 denaria" or something like $750 (§6). But it was so concentrated that only a few drops (mixed with a quantity of olive oil) were used at a time, and the one jar might have lasted the woman all her life; in her grief at the prospect of Jesus' death, however, she poured it all on His head as the only offering she could make Him.

This story is often confused with that of §95 but the two have very little in common.

204

The Last Supper may have been either the actual Passover or some anticipatory meal held the evening before; Jesus' words can be understood in either sense. The Passover commemorated the Jews' redemption from Egypt (Exodus 12: 1-14, etc.), and its spiritual "fulfillment" will take place in the final redemption brought by God's Kingdom. For the pictorial language compare §144.

The use of wine at the Passover (and other Jewish religious meals) was not directed in the Old Testament, but was a later addition to symbolize joy. For Jesus at that moment its use would therefore have been unfitting; but He insisted that His disciples should drink, since His death was for their unspeakable benefit (§205).

205

As bread is broken and wine poured out to feed men, so the death of Jesus brings them spiritual life. "Blood of the covenant" looks back to Exodus 24: 8; a new relation between God and man was about to be inaugurated.

No definition of the nature of this "covenant" was given, however: Jesus simply stated the fact. And that the fact is true every disciple of Jesus knows.

The words used when Jesus pronounced the thanksgivings were almost certainly: "Blessed be thou, O Lord, King of the universe, who bringest forth bread from the ground," and "Blessed be thou, O Lord, King of the universe, who createst the fruit of the vine."

206

For the fulfillment of God's purpose the death of Jesus was necessary—but not the treachery of Judas.

Whether "son of man" here means "man" ("this man," "I") as in §§53, 120 or "Messiah" as in §210, etc., cannot be determined; perhaps Jesus meant Judas to take the former sense while He Himself thought of the latter.

207

Even yet the disciples had much to learn (§§195, 198).

208

The missionaries could no longer look forward (§119) to short journeys in a country where hospitality could be taken for granted. The "sword" would be needed primarily as a protection against wild animals.

209

Such distress could never have been caused by mere dread of physical suffering; what made His death terrible to Jesus was that it proved His people's moral degradation and their rejection of God.

Peter had already forgotten the warning of §207.

210

When Israel's high priest asked Jesus the supreme question, He could no longer remain silent. But His description of His own destiny is simply quoted from the prophets' predictions (a combination of Daniel 7: 13 and Psalm 110: 1; compare §202).

211-219

For the interpretation of these sayings compare §70. The Jews were so fixed in their belief that the end of the world was at hand (§a), that it was only in this language that they could conceive the frightful catastrophe about to fall on

Jerusalem and on the nation (§211; compare §74, etc.). In any case this catastrophe was the fearful example of God's judgments forever on peoples and on individuals.

212

The Jews spent endless time on ingenious schemes for computing when the end would come, and in searching for special "signs" of its approach. But God gives men no such exact warnings of His judgments; when they come, they come suddenly and it is too late for guilty souls to escape.

A traditional rendition of the last line is "The Kingdom of God is in your hearts," as if the Kingdom were only a matter of right inner attitude. But this rendition is wrong.

213

The prophecies quoted in §210 are fulfilled at Jesus' death; from thenceforth God's judgments are His judgments also.

214-215

Although no precise computation of the time of the Judgment was possible (§211), there were moral signs that showed it was impending and that it could not be long delayed (§73, etc.). But God alone knew the "day" and "hour."

216

The disciples are warned not to long for their reward when there was work to be done.

217

In this saying the meaning of "these things" is not precisely given, but the sense must be much the same as that of §73.

218

Compare §212. The references are to Genesis 7 and 19.

219-220

The Judgment was often pictured as falling only on the non-Jews. But there will be no distinction of any sort; judgment will fall wherever it finds an object.

"Taken" is probably "delivered."

221

The end returns to the beginning (§§1-2), with the results of love and of selfishness now fully declared.

INDEXES

INDEX I

TO BIBLICAL PASSAGES

Parentheses enclose passages in which the parallel is not close.
Brackets enclose passages that are probably later additions to the
Biblical text.

a Mk 1: 4-6 = Lk 3: 2b-3 = Mt
  3: 1-2, 4-6.
  Lk 3: 7-9 = Mt 3: 7-10.
  Lk 3: 16-17 = Mt 3: 11-12.

b Mk 1: 9-11 = Lk 3: 21-22 =
  Mt 3: 13, 16-17.

c Lk 4: 1-12 = Mt 4: 1-10. (Mk
  1: 12-13).

1 Mk 12: 28-31 = Mt 22: 34-40
  (Lk 10: 25-28).

2a Mt 5: 17.

2b Mt 7: 12 = Lk 6: 31.

3 Mt 5: 43-45 (Lk 6: 27-28).

4 Mt 5: 46-48 (Lk 6: 32, 33,
  36)

5 Lk 6: 32-35 (Mt 5: 46-47).

6 Lk 10: 29-37.

7 Lk 13: 30 (Mk 10: 31 = Mt
  19: 30; Mt 20: 16).

8 Lk 14: 11; Lk 18: 14b; Mt
  18: 4; 23: 12.

9 Mt 7: 1-2 = Lk 6: 37a, 38b
  (Mk 4: 24b).

10 Mt 7: 3-5 = Lk 6: 41-42.

11 Lk 17: 7-10.

12 Mt 5: 21-22.

13 Mt 5: 23-24.

14 Mt 6: 12 = Lk 11: 4a.

15 Mt 6: 14-15 (Mk 11: 25-
  [26]).

16 Lk 17: 3-4 (Mt 18: 15, 21-22).

17 Mt 18: 21-22 (Lk 17: 4).

18 Mt 5: 38-41 (Lk 6: 29-30).

19 Lk 6: 37-38.

20 Lk 9: 52-55.

21 Mt 18: 23-35.

22 Lk 12: 15.

23 Mt 5: 42 (Lk 6: 30).

24 Mt 6: 24 = Lk 16: 13.

25 Mt 6: 19-21 (Lk 12: 33-34).

26 Lk 14: 12-14.

27 Lk 12: 16-20.

28 Mk 12: 41-44 = Lk 21: 1-4.

29 Mt 5: 33-37.

30 Mt 23: 20-22.

31 Mt 5: 27-28.

32 Mk 10: 2-9 = Mt 19: 3-8.

33 Lk 6: 45 = Mt 12: 34b-35.

34 Lk 6: 43, 44 = Mt 7: 16-18
  (Mt 12: 33).

35 Mt 6: 22-23 = Lk 11: 34.

36 Mt 13: 44.

37 Mt 13: 45-46.

38 Mt 7: 13-14 (Lk 13: 24).

39 Mk 10: 25 = Lk 18: 25 = Mt
  19: 24.

40 Mk 10: 17-22 = Lk 18: 18-
  23 = Mt 19: 16-22.

41 Lk 16: 1-8.

42 Mt 18: 7.

43 Mk 9: 43-47 = Mt 18: 8-9
  (Mt 5: 29-30).

44 Lk 12: 13-14.

45 Mk 12: 13-17 = Lk 20: 20-25
  = Mt 22: 15-22.

46 Mt 5: 3-10 (Lk 6: 20-21).

47 Mk 7: 15 = Mt 15: 11.

48 Mt 23: 24.

49 Mt 23: 23 = Lk 11: 42.

50 Mt 23: 25-26.

51 Lk 11: 38-40.
52 Mt 23: 16-19.
53 Mk 2: 27-28 (Lk 6: 5 = Mt 12: 8).
54 Mk 3: 4 = Lk 6: 9 (Mt 12: 12b).
55 Lk 14: 5 = Mt 12: 11-12a.
56 Mk 2: 23-26 = Lk 6: 1-4 = Mt 12: 1-4.
57 Mt 12: 5-7 (Mt 9: 13a).
58 Mk 7: 9-13a = Mt 15: 3-6.
59a Lk 11: 46 (Mt 23: 4).
59b Lk 11: 52 (Mt 23: 13).
60 Lk 11: 44.
61 Mt 23: 27.
62 Mt 23: 15.
63 Mt 23: 29-31 (Lk 11: 47-48a).
64 Mk 12: 38-40 = Lk 20: 46-47 (Mt 23: 6-7a, [14]; Lk 11: 43).
65 Mt 21: 31b.
66 Mt 15: 14b = Lk 6: 39b.
67 Lk 12: 1 (Mk 8: 15 = Mt 16: 6).
68 Mt 5: 20.
69 Mt 7: 15-18, 20 (Lk 6: 43-44; Mt 12: 33).
70 Mt 4: 17 (Mk 1: 15).
71 Mk 8: 36 = Lk 9: 25 = Mt 16: 26.
72 Lk 12: 58-59 (Mt 5: 25-26).
73 Lk 12: 54-56 (Mt [16: 2-3]).
74 Lk 13: 1-5.
75 Lk 16: 19-31.
76 Mk 4: 9 = Lk 8: 8b = Mt 13: 9; Mk 4: 23; Mt 11: 15; Mt 13: 43b; Lk 14: 35b.
77 Lk 6: 46 (Mt 7: 21).
78 Lk 12: 47-48a.
79 Lk 12: 48b.
80 Lk 16: 10.
81 Lk 19: 26 = Mt 25: 29 (Mk 4: 25 = Lk 8: 18; Mt 13: 12).

82 Mt 25: 14-28a (Lk 19: 12-24a).
83 Lk 11: 24-26 = Mt 12: 43-45.
84 Mt 25: 13 (Mt 24: 42; Mk 13: 35).
85 Mt 24: 43 = Lk 12: 39.
86 Mt 25: 1-12 (Lk 13: 25).
87 Mt 7: 24-27 = Lk 6: 47-49.
88 Mk 10: 13-15 = Lk 18: 15-17 = Mt 19: 13-14; 18: 3.
89 Lk 18: 10-14a.
90 Mt 21: 28-31.
91 Mt 20: 1-15.
92 Mk 2: 14 = Lk 5: 27-28 = Mt 9: 9.
93 Mk 2: 16-17a = Lk 5: 30-31 = Mt 9: 11-12.
94 Lk 19: 2-9.
95 Lk 7: 36-43.
96 Lk 15: 4-7 = Mt 18: 12-14.
97 Lk 15: 8-10.
98 Lk 15: 11-32.
99 Mt 6: 1-6, 16-18.
100 Lk 11: 2-4 = Mt 6: 9-13.
101 Lk 11: 9-10 = Mt 7: 7-8.
102 Lk 11: 11-13 = Mt 7: 9-11.
103 Mt 6: 7-8.
104 Lk 11: 5-8.
105 Lk 18: 1-5.
106 Lk 18: 27 = Mk 10: 27 = Mt 19: 26.
107 Mk 11: 24 = Mt 21: 22.
108 Mt 17: 20 = Lk 17: 6 (Mk 9: 23; Mk 11: 23 = Mt 21: 21).
109 Mt 6: 34.
110 Lk 12: 22-31 = Mt 6: 25-33.
111 Lk 10: 38-42.
112 Mk 12: 18-27 = Lk 20: 27-38 = Mt 22: 23-32.
113 Mt 11: 28-30.
114 Lk 10: 2 = Mt 9: 37-38.
115 Mk 1: 16-20 = Mt 4: 18-22 (Lk 5: 10-11).
116 Mk 2: 14 = Lk 5: 27-28 = Mt 9: 9.

117 Mk 3: 16-19 = Lk 6: 14-16 = Mt 10: 2-4.
118 Mk 8: 34 = Lk 9: 23 = Mt 16: 24.
119 Lk 10: 4a = Lk 9: 3 = Mt 10: 9-10a = Mk 6: 8.
120 Lk 9: 57-58 = Mt 8: 19-20.
121 Lk 9: 59-60 = Mt 8: 21-22.
122 Lk 9: 61-62.
123 Mk 10: 21-22 = Lk 18: 22-23 = Mt 19: 21-22.
124 Mt 19: 12.
125 Lk 14: 28-30.
126 Lk 14: 31-33.
127 Mt 10: 24-25 (Lk 6: 40).
128 Mt 10: 34-36 (Lk 12: 51-53).
129 Mt 10: 37 (Lk 14: 26).
130 Mt 10: 17-18 (Mk 13: 9; Lk 21: 12).
131 Mt 5: 14b.
132 Lk 12: 3 = Mt 10: 27.
133 Lk 12: 2 = Mt 10: 26 (Mk 4: 22 = Lk 8: 17).
134 Mt 5: 13 (Lk 14: 34-35; Mk 9: 50).
135 Mt 5: 14a, 15-16 (Lk 11: 33; Mk 4: 21 = Lk 8: 16).
136 Mt 10: 28 = Lk 12: 4-5.
137 Mt 10: 39 (Mk 8: 35 = Lk 9: 24 = Mt 16: 25; Lk 17: 33).
138 Lk 12: 8-9 = Mt 10: 32-33 (Mk 8: 38 = Lk 9: 26).
139 Mk 2: 18-19a, 21-22 = Lk 5: 33-34, 36-37 = Mt 9: 14-15a, 16-17.
140 Mt 5: 11-12 (Lk 6: 22-23).
141 Lk 12: 6-7 = Mt 10: 29-31.
142 Mk 10: 29-30 = Lk 18: 29-30 = Mt 19: 29.
143 Mt 10: 19-20 = Lk 12: 11-12 (Mk 13: 11 = Lk 21: 14-15).
144 Lk 22: 28-30 = Mt 19: 28.
145 Lk 10: 4b.

146 Mt 10: 5-6.
147 Lk 10: 5-6 = Mt 10: 12-13.
148 Lk 10: 7a, c = Mt 10: 11b (Mk 6: 10 = Lk 9: 4).
149 Lk 10: 7b = Mt 10: 10b.
150 Mt 10: 16 = Lk 10: 3.
151 Mt 7: 6.
152 Mt 13: 52.
153 Lk 7: 35 = Mt 11: 19b.
154 Lk 10: 16 (Mt 10: 40).
155 Lk 8: 5-8a = Mk 4: 3-8 = Mt 13: 3-8.
156 Mt 13: 47-48.
157 Mk 1: 35-38 = Lk 4: 42-43.
158 Mk 6: 1-4 = Mt 13: 54-57 (Lk 4: 16a, 22, 24).
159 Mt 11: 12-13 = Lk 16: 16.
160 Lk 5: 39.
161 Mt 11: 2-11 = Lk 7: 19-28.
162 Lk 11: 29-30 = Mt 12: 38-39 (Mk 8: 12 = Mt 16: 4).
163 Lk 11: 23 = Mt 12: 30.
164 Lk 12: 10 = Mt 12: 32 (Mk 3: 28-29).
165 Lk 7: 31-34 = Mt 11: 16-19a.
166 Lk 11: 15, 17-20 = Mt 12: 24-28 = Mk 3: 23-26.
167 Lk 13: 6-9.
168 Lk 13: 29-30 = Mt 8: 11; Mt 19: 30 = Mt 20: 16 = Mk 10: 31.
169 Lk 13: 28 = Mt 8: 11b-12.
170 Lk 11: 31-32 = Mt 12: 42-41.
171 Lk 10: 10-12 = Mt 10: 14-15 (Mk 6: 11 = Lk 9: 5).
172 Lk 10: 13-14 = Mt 11: 21-22.
173 Mt 11: 23-24 = Lk 10: 15.
174 Lk 14: 16-21 (Mt 22: 1-10).
175 Mk 12: 1-5, 9 = Lk 20: 9-12, 15b-16a = Mt 21: 33-36, 41.
176 Lk 10: 16a (Mt 10: 40a).
177 Mk 3: 35 = Lk 8: 21 = Mt 12: 50 (Lk 11: 27-28).
178 Mt 10: 40-42 (Mk 9: 41).

179   Mk 9: 36-37 = Lk 9: 47-48a (Mt 18: 5).

180   Mk 9: 42 = Mt 18: 6 (Lk 17: 1-2).

181   Mk 9: 38-39 = Lk 9: 49-50a.

182   Lk 22: 25-26 = Mk 10: 42-44 = Mt 20: 25-27 (Mk 9: 35 = Lk 9: 48b; Mt 23: 11).

183   Lk 12: 42-46 = Mt 24: 45-51a.

184   Mk 7: 25-29 = Mt 15: 22-28a.

185   Mt 8: 5-10 = Lk 7: 2, 6-9.

186   Lk 10: 23-24 = Mt 13: 16-17.

187   Lk 11: 20 = Mt 12: 28.

188   Lk 11: 21-22 = Mt 12: 29 = Mk 3: 27.

189   Lk 10: 17-20.

190   Lk 10: 21-22 = Mt 11: 25-27.

191   Lk 7: 28 = Mt 11: 11.

192   Mk 4: 26-29.

193   Lk 13: 18-19 = Mt 13: 31-32 = Mk 4: 30-32.

194   Lk 13: 20-21 = Mt 13: 33.

195   Mk 8: 27-33 = Lk 9: 18-22 = Mt 16: 13-16, 20-23.

196   Lk 12: 49-50.

197   Lk 13: 31-33.

198   Mk 10: 35-40 = Mt 20: 20-23.

199   Mk 11: 1-10 = Lk 19: 28-38 = Mt 21: 1-9.

200   Mk 11: 15-17 = Lk 19: 45-46 = Mt 21: 12-13.

201   Mk 11: 27-33 = Lk 20: 1-8 = Mt 21: 23-27.

202   Mk 12: 35-37a = Lk 20: 41-44 = Mt 22: 41-45.

203   Mk 14: 3-7 = Mt 26: 6-11.

204   Lk 22: 15-18 = Mk 14: 25 = Mt 26: 29.

205   Mk 14: 22-24 = Mt 26: 26-28 = Lk 19a, [19b-20].

206   Mk 14: 20-21 = Mt 26: 23-24 = Lk 22: 21-22.

207   Mk 14: 29-30 = Mt 26: 33-34 = Lk 22: 33-34.

208   Lk 22: 35-36.

209   Mk 14: 32-38 = Mt 26: 36-41 = Lk 22: 40-42, 45-46.

210   Mk 14: 62 = Mt 26: 64 = Lk 22: 69.

211   Mk 13: 1-2 = Mt 24: 1-2 = Lk 21: 5-6 (Lk 19: 43-44).

212   Lk 17: 20-21 (Lk 17: 23 = Mt 24: 26; Mk 13: 21 = Mt 24: 23).

213   Mt 24: 27 = Lk 17: 24.

214   Mk 13: 30 = Mt 24: 34 = Lk 21: 32 (Mk 9: 1 = Mt 16: 28 = Lk 9: 27; Mt 10: 23).

215   Mk 13: 32 = Mt 24: 36.

216   Lk 17: 22.

217   Mk 13: 28-29 = Mt 24: 32-33 = Lk 21: 29-31.

218   Lk 17: 26-29 = Mt 24: 37-39.

219   Mt 24: 40-41 = Lk 17: 34-35, [36].

220   Lk 17: 37b = Mt 24: 28.

221   Mt 25: 31-46.

INDEX II

137

MARK

LUKE

GENERAL INDEX

For terms of frequent occurrence reference is given only to the more significant passages or to the section in which the meaning is explained.

142